The Grassling

ELIZABETH-JANE BURNETT

The Grassling

A Geological Memoir

ALLEN LANE
an imprint of
PENGUIN BOOKS

ALLEN LANE

UK | USA | Canada | Ireland | Australia
India | New Zealand | South Africa

Penguin
Random House
UK

Allen Lane is part of the Penguin Random House group of companies
whose addresses can be found at global.penguinrandomhouse.com

First published 2019
001

Set in 10.2/14.25 pt Sabon LT Pro by Integra Software Services Pvt. Ltd, Pondicherry
Printed in Great Britain by Clays Ltd, Elcograf S.p.A.

A CIP catalogue record for this book is available from the British Library

ISBN: 978-0-241-37412-2

Contents

CONTENTS

The thin layer of soil that forms a patchy covering over the continents controls our own existence and that of every other animal of
the land. Without soil, land plants as we know them could not
grow, and without plants no animals could survive.

Yet if our agriculture-based life depends on the soil, it is equally
true that soil depends on life, its very origins and the maintenance of
its true nature being intimately related to living plants and animals.

Rachel Carson, *Silent Spring*

Plant bioacoustics is a newly emerged field of plant communication.
Plants produce sound waves in the lower end of the audio range as
well as an overabundance of ultrasonic sounds. By capturing the
signals emitted by plants under different environmental conditions,
I am exploring the ecological significance of these sounds to communication among plants and between plants and other organisms.

Monica Gagliano, 'Plant Communication'

'What a strange noise the leaves of the trees make,' he said. 'It's as
if they were talking to one another – telling secrets.'

'Wisha-wisha-wisha-wisha,' whispered the trees.

'They *are* telling secrets,' said Beth. 'And do you know, Rick – if
the trees have any message for us, we can hear it by pressing our left
ears to the trunks of the trees! Then we *really* hear what they say.'

Enid Blyton, *The Magic Faraway Tree*, Book 2

BEFORE

On the shortest day, the light never ends. Conifers buffer deep gusts of air, animals cry. The sky stings of a metal or an ore; iron wool rolled flat from moon to field. No stars. Clouds ripple the darkening grey. It must be darker because colours are, but the feeling is still of light. The body and the air. Coming back to the place you know: particular trees, the same grass, the ground you have known all your life – this is in the air. This is in the cloud. This is what the eyes follow, long after there is anything to see. Ice immerses skin, hair, nail. There is no touching in this tundra, nothing can bear to. This could be a place without speech. Where no lips part. Were it not for the traces of cries in the sodden air, in the slow beat of tarpaulin over hay, gathering moonlight in the black of its flaps. No animals. Except in echoes. Hundreds of years could pass like this. With this wind, ice and blank air, hollowed of pulse and paw. Not the longest night, but the slowest light. Stars begin. Pools of moon bathe the leaves. The ice takes any beating heart.

The light is phenomenal. Clear, pristine, unfiltered. Ghosts dance in the tarpaulin. I sleep in and out of the moon. The day is always here. It is just behind the night. Clouds are urgent, the speech of the wind is feathered but strong and when the light doesn't call it is wind. Battering against me, 'Wake, wake, open! Come apart and open.' Tonight is not for sleeping. It is for loosening the parts of yourself you forget in the daytime. It is for remembering that you are a force that goes on in spite of yourself. That you do not stop when you sleep. That you are not at rest when there is fury and sound in you, stretching the day clean out of its hours. And finally, when light and ice have passed beyond human tolerance, when it cannot be borne, when you are nearly lost and you almost accept it, there is morning.

Geese exit trees. Ducks fly over, not stopping. Willows stand lean: pure limb. It is then that I miss the vegetables. What would it take to dig this ground again? Muscles I don't have, sinew I don't own and the time to be here. Standing in the middle of the plot, thinking platitudes about change and how the soil shows this more than anything, I see it. A single rose bending over the ground; its light lemon is the sun of a hundred mornings and I still see the packet my father used as a marker under the stubs of dead branches, 'Gloire de Dijon', a climbing rose.

Nearby, the great beech, whose fall I saw last September, has joined a lattice of underlying branches, flattened to form a human nest. It calls out to be climbed. An aphid moves along ivy under my hands, which are tools now, propelling me. Everything slips. Rain gathers in upturned leaves; smooth bark has no traction. I reach the nest in seconds. A moment's pause as I assess whether or not the branch that forms its spine can hold me. It could splinter and so could my legs, my shoulders.

When he fell, it was not from anything as stupid as climbing trees. Yet I want to risk it. To sit on the spine and fall back, head in branch; to look up, cradled by wood. But the branches themselves seem to speak, to coax me back. 'We cannot bear you. We cannot help you.' And I know they are right. I edge backwards down the trunk: so easy to climb, treacherous to descend. Feet find no hold; jumper rucks up and bark on belly is cold, as leaves are, to the skin. I have no choice but to relax: tension bears a weight that unsteadies. Muscles retract enough to make subtle negotiations of buttock over hip, the swing of both legs over, until only pelvis touches wood. I jump and land. Sound leaps.

Wood cracks as it's split apart for logs. The thump of it falls into barrow; the shuffle and slide of things being put into their proper place. Over it all a light 'tseep tseep' as little birds fall in from wherever they have been. And as the day drains, the sounds of the world close. Engines end; dogs quiet; squirrels' purrs edge

under fur. Insects slow their clicks. Staggered hoots and deep lowing. More than the day is ending. Evening fire dulled to pastel,
dusting over hedges. Moon-gasp. Electric orb fringed by firs. That
great moon going on. A perfect round, pulsing to the bat flicker,
trickle river. That great continuing. Glow.

ONE

I

Acreage

Tonight the light from the cottage on the hill is the last to go, as the rain beats against the windows. Pulled and pummelled, I wake somewhere in the storm; where, somehow, there is singing. In the wide blast of rain, a twinkle of sound chimes its resistance. In the short respites from the wind, sudden darts as chaffinch, blackbird, bullfinch get where they need to go, like people running for cover in the rain. The eightieth year after my father was born is a strong one: bullish, stamping its way through the calendar. It is a night full of fight and I hope some of it reaches him; that he breathes in deeply and is charged. I can't tell if the rain has stopped or is just part of me now, but it falls like a blessing and I sleep.

In the morning, rain coats as thick as a pelt, as I stay out completing my fieldwork: my inventory of the night, and the deer, and the time since I was last here. The word 'acreage' denotes arable land, though is not necessarily measured in acres. But here, where the field is an acre in size, the word encompasses the field. An acre of age, where prints of all description are held in the ground: the heavy hoof of deer; lighter treads of badger and rabbit. They press the soil with little animal touches. Some soil is dispersed, caught in the ridges of hooves, in clumps of fur – only to re-settle a little further off. Some is nourished, with manure from their tactile bodies. And the bodies, in turn, feed from the soil, picking plants whose roots stretch across the first few inches. And so this has gone on for centuries, this lifting and falling of the earth by the lifting and falling of paws. So this gentle ploughing continues. As I look into this patch of ground, I wonder how long it has been there, where it came from, when and where it will go. Lately, I have been questioning many things I used to take for granted; that I used to think would always be there.

I run to the copse for cover, crying out as I slip in the soft mud, sending a racket of pheasants up. Trees creak and sway above, clashing branches like antlers. The sound of the wood is a fire, everywhere catching alight. Bird nests lurch high in the wind, their inhabitants facing the bends and swerves of a blustery roller-coaster. I follow the deer I have missed, by Mum's report, by two days. I sense where they broke through: two gaps in the hedge I crawl towards. Crouching down to the tracks, I find myself at eye level with clumps of elderberries. I stand in the stream, my head level with the land above, eyes full of ivy and deadly nightshade. A tunnel runs away from me, a highway for small animals. I have stumbled on a little town of voles, a thoroughfare for tiny feet. To the left, an exposed tree root twists like a bone: a knee joint or elbow, covered with moss glowing high green in the dappled sun. Strips of tree lie loosely attached, pulled out by the wind.

Then it sounds like the wood itself is speaking. It is hard to tell the creak of the wood from the squeak of the bird. Other little birds fall in around the noise: thrushes, wrens, robins, but it remains unseen. It seems like the bark is tearing open, pouring its sounded sap onto the twigs below. Then nothing. Periods of intense activity fall away as quickly as they came. As I head towards the house, red bursts through the winter rose. It rips through the rosebud cherry, the cotoneaster, the Martin's spurge I pick to take to the hospital. The hedge roars. The orange dogwood, also known as 'midwinter fire', calls out to be taken too. It is a fierce flare of a garden. I am still here, it shouts. There is no arguing with its presence.

In the evening, he rallies. The last sun flutters him over like a blackbird. Our eyes follow the leaves brought from his acre out over the sideboard, past the curtain, the sliding doors, the city's walls;

back to the place we have known all our lives. There, clouds end in bullfinch pink. Slices of hot colour peel from the sky, exposing the soft air beneath. Crumbling like charcoal to the grass, the colours fall. A bird ticks into stillness and we breathe.

*

The soil that my father's fathers farmed lies in the Devon village of Ide. As I plan a return to this soil, I find I am increasingly guided by its Celtic layers. The mapping of these settlements seems to have preoccupied my father, who authored a local history of the village, A History of the People and Parish of Ide. The book includes a linguistic tracking, following the derivations of place names.

I am conducting fieldwork in this village and in my father's present home of Stockleigh Pomeroy and corresponding with him about it. I operate in twenty-four-hour marathons slipped in between teaching in Birmingham, making notes on the back of shopping lists and around the borders of tissues. This may not be quite what early topographers like William of Camden envisioned when they encouraged later writers to continue their work. Camden's Britannia, the first chorographical survey of the islands of Great Britain and Ireland, explored the Celtic tribal areas within the counties' boundaries. Yet his methodology, a mix of archival and anecdotal research, is not so dissimilar to mine; though to his maps and records I add scribbled observations, feelings, phonemes: little edges of words that poke out from the landscape, that shoot up from the pit of language. For oral testimony, I start to wonder who else might be speaking. What might the grass tell of the ground? Or worms, of earth? Could the soil itself speak?

I take up my father's History and come to rest on a sketch map at the back: 'Field Names near the Dunchideock Boundary'. It is the focus on the names that intoxicates, that sends me shooting back through time, wrapped in the language of the fields. Based on an 1803 Survey Map of the Manor, the sketch shows a division of land that has been in place for at least two hundred years, with the field names tracked back further. In his *History*, my father asks of the fields First, Second and Third Drewshill, 'Is it fanciful to see the names of these fields as a corruption of "Druid's Hill", i.e. "the hill of the priest"?'

'No,' I breathe.

'This would be further indication that this was a religious site in pre-Roman times, and what is more –'

'Yes?'

'– continued as such, long into the Saxon period, as, otherwise –'

'Yes?'

'– the name . . . would not have survived.'

Weeks pass before I can reach Druid's Hill and I have to make do with virtual visits from Birmingham. Navigating online, I come quickly to Exeter and, from there, pass on to Ide, home of the Druid. I float over what I think are the Drewshill fields and wonder about their size. I zoom out to compare them with their neighbours. The second Drewshill looks compact, nestled between the others. It seems filled with grass, but a lighter shade than those around it. I wonder if it holds a different species, or if it's just at a different stage of maturity. Who does it feed, I wonder. Who grows in it?

I flick across to my own village, where my father is now, and chart our house where it lies in its acreage; aerial zooming through a human hawk-eye. The rush of affection at seeing a field I have known since childhood beam down electrodes to where I sit in an unknown city – as I become a yellow stickman avatar, wandering the country lanes I am too far from to walk in person – is startling. I see the neighbouring farms, and the different tones of their fields. Because I know them, I know what each colour means: potatoes, carrots, onions, swedes. And I know some of the people they are feeding and have encountered birds and insects who grow there too. I wonder about a map that could go deeper into these fields, that could tell me what's there, how it feels and what it has to say.

Yet even at this surface level, the map bears a kind of thrill. When W. G. Hoskins said in *The Making of the English Landscape*, 'There are certain sheets of the one-inch Ordnance Survey maps which one can sit down and read like a book for an hour on end, with growing pleasure and imaginative excitement,' he had yet to encounter Google Maps. I am completely immersed, swooping over the landscape. Now I see it as if from an aeroplane, a rolling patchwork of greens. You can drag and drop this avatar; fly in from Birmingham, down into the specific field you are looking for. Day after day I hover over one landscape, while living in another.

During this time, I dream deeply of the earth: men in armour, women fading in and out of focus. I dream of boundary lines and farmers telling me which people belong to which earth. Whether it is one acre, or thirty, or hundreds, the sense of ownership is the same; the sense of self so deeply tangled in the soil that it is impossible to say who owns who. Pointing out the hedgerow and the channel of earth that runs beside it, the dream segues into another, earlier one I have had about swimming, where the river is nothing more than a ribbon along a hedge for miles until I find the right spot, where it deepens into what looks like an actual place I know on the river Exe – only the dream version is magnified into a perfect pool. Submerged, I taste the water, the weeds and the soil in the water. There are people and fish I seem to know, swimming towards me. While we are from different species, other centuries, it's not too unsettling, just like meeting cousins you've only met once or twice, or relatives of your best friends. As I break the surface of the river and the dream I gasp: what fills my lungs is wider than breath could be. It is a place and a language torn, matted and melded; flowered and chiming with bones. That breath is that place and until I get there I will not really be breathing.

2

Burnett

As I puff up Pole House Lane, my father's words ring through the hedges. *Presumably not many Ideites today would be very keen on walking to the top of Pole House Lane every time they wanted to attend a function.* According to his speculation, the first settlement of what later became Ide parish may have been here, where this road meets Markham Lane. A heavy-set farmer brushes past in a van, sending me into the brambles. I glimpse a ruddy face and snowing hair. *Would my father have known him,* I think, *would he have known my father?* Spotted with cuckoo spit, the hedges glow, and for the first time this winter I see that it is spring. Breathing in buttercups, their soft warmth nestles in my throat, brightening the body.

But when I reach Druid's Hill, I deflate. High hedges obscure it; here and there a glimpse of grass; no flowers, no rivers, no dreams. Consulting the sketch map from my father's book I see the three fields that take the name of a Druid and move onto the one now called Second Drewshill. No better. By the time I reach Third Drewshill, I have abandoned all romantic place names in my notes, reducing them to Field 1, Field 2, Field 3.

> Field 1: Blank grass.
> Field 2: Rough green.
> Field 3: Snatches of orange and brown.

I walk up and down the lane, repeating my inventory. Everywhere closed off, inaccessible, still as stone. I wonder who or what could tell me anything here. What is the sound of these quiet places?

Field 1: Deep inhale of wren. Lichen and thorn.
Field 2: There is something here. There is something and it is in the smell, pulling me down through the soil.
Field 3: Purple tufts draw me in, off-road, illicit territory. A tractor's roar over the hedge puts me on edge while the earth holds me here. Sprigs of sheep's wool, summoning.

As I return to Field 1, I begin to doubt if it is even the right field. In a new place my heart leaps and feet fly before I can hold them back and it is always these parts of the body that navigate. I usually get a sense of a place, finding my way by hunch, hunch becoming habit, and that is how I get anywhere.

Field 2: As I try to fall down, connect with whatever is here beneath eye level, a nearby tractor emerges and stops me in my tracks. I belong because of my father: tracing his footsteps, his ancestors; following their trail of dusted bone. I don't belong because of time. I don't know who farms this land now. I can't see in. So much is snatched glimpses and long thin paths – I want a flat, open moment.

Field 3: Looking down, the field further in is brown and yellow like moorland. Though it calls me, I know it is not what I am looking for.

Field 4: Churchills, on the opposite side of the lane. My father cites Allen Mawer as revealing the prefix 'church' in the name 'Churchills' to be a corruption of the Celtic word '*crich*', meaning burial mound. *If this is so, then Churchills was once a sacred place.* There is a footpath here, so I can reach further in. In the quiet, without the tractor, it is possible to imagine reaching it – whatever is here, contained. But this busyness is part of the land now; the spiritual pushed out, or at least back and fenced off.

Reaching Markham Lane in blustery mood, I continue my hedge

assessment. At the corner, something sparkles. Craning in, I find the plastic lid of a Tupperware box. I flick the lid off eagerly, to a cluster of coordinates and dates. I have stumbled upon a geocache. From Celtic to contemporary in one sweep of a hedge. Instead of adding the usual information, I write some garbled message about researching the area for historical purposes, signing off proudly: 'BURNETT'. It feels good to leave *this* name in *this* hedge.

Names as mantras repeat through the generations: places for people (hill for Druid), people for places (Druid for hill), until the thing we conjure by uttering is so much an amalgamation that we cannot split the person from the place, the man or woman from the field. Though I have not been here long, the seconds feel stretched out, as they always are, by love. And that is what has brought me here; this I know, though I do not yet quite understand.

As I have not given much thought to what to do after finding Druid's Hill, I go first one way up Markham Lane, then the other, all the while continuing my border patrol. Through the hedge's holes I see a different texture: rough stubble rising from mud. Where the plough has zigzagged the earth like afro hair being straightened, its tracks are a comb's teeth pulling through a gloop of chemicals. And as the scalp stings and prickles with heat, so the land burns and the mice run and the beetles break and the worms forget themselves in the newness of sliced bodies.

But they carry on. They send their bristles out to the displaced soil and hold. Thicken each of their five hearts, pumping their human blood with the haemoglobin that has no right to be there. Burrow and consume, extracting life from dying leaves as their tunnels form soil pores, letting oxygen and water in, carbon dioxide out. Break down roots and stems and sunken seeds so that bacteria and fungi can feed and release their nutrients; mix soil layers dispersing organic matter through like a soft soil wind for bacteria, fungi and plants; fertilizing the very ends of the follicles. They are in the surface compost, in the middle ground tunnels, in permanent burrows deep below; tiny travellers, carrying nutrients and minerals from beneath the ground to its surface, breaking the boundary between elements.

Completely obscured, I peer through tangles of taut twig. To my left, the white head of the Haldon Belvedere pokes up from forest like a white hart with its ears pricked up. Its presence breathes a living history on a hill. They are everywhere, these ghosts, if we only have the time and quiet to see them. A grey face peeps out from the hedge and before I have registered it for what it is, it's gone, back down the rabbit hole. There, but not seen, ghost rabbits running through the margins. Through a twig-gap I glimpse Exeter as the boom of the A30 washes over the grass. Swimming in traffic, I fall back into the swerve of a man on a bike and both of us tangle together in the shock of each other's presences.

'Sorry, I wasn't looking,' he says.

'Neither was I,' I realize my eyes had been closed and my hands had been writing with half my head in a hedge.

I turn back to earth. The magnetism of the land, not just where I was birthed, but where my father was; his father and his; pulls me to it, as if by knowing it, I should know them. Should I believe it? It has no reason to lie. Passing back through the years is like when the 'I' becomes detached and you're aware of a life outside of yourself, looking down at you, incredulous that the 'I' should be this small body going about its business, looking so plausible. Like that, but further in. As though, if you exercised this muscle, you could get there; could feel the land as it was then, the names that lived then; find yourself hovering over some other body, some other body's life. With apparent ease I flow backwards – not flow, it is less bodied than that – melt, from Churchills to *crich* to burial mound; from Drewshill to Druid's Hill to the hill of the priest.

And what happens to the land through these human cycles? What is two thousand years in the span of the soil? Is any part of the earth I touch now the earth that lived then, with the bodies of my family, my grandparents and their parents and a billion other organisms, for there are billions of organisms in one handful.

Yet the layers of soil stay much the same in one human lifetime, unless moved or scraped or ploughed. Unless a blow to the head, or a blade, blunts the billions of lives inside you.

I want to hear the stories of the soil; not just as human support, or as host, but as consciousness linked to a place always, unless moved by another (wind, water, ice, gravity). Do you want to move, but have to wait for others to move you; or want to stay but have no say in it? I want to know if you're overpopulated; if it all gets too much and if so, where do you go? Do you have favourites? Particular roots or burrowing animals who treat you well and softly?

I cannot comprehend you all at once. Your spreading and latticing; binding and breathing; dispersing and filtering; degrading and detoxifying; eating, excreting, breaking, exchanging, morphing; it is exhausting just to think of you.

*

I tell my father about the fields. It is difficult for him to move now, yet I am sure I found something of him there. Could he, perhaps, have a secret life? At night, when we think him sleeping, could he suddenly recover the energy of youth and strike out across country, nine miles, back to the village of his boyhood, to the fields of his grandfather?

He thinks they once formed part of Woolmans farm, where his grandfather Frank was a labourer. He thinks it strange that I should ask so much about them.

'But isn't it interesting,' I say, 'about their names?'

'Yes, I've always thought so,' he replies.

'And what did you say Burnett means?' He's told me many times, but somehow I never remember.

'*Beornhard. Beorn* meaning warrior in Anglo-Saxon.'

'Yes, warrior,' I repeat, and sit with him until he sleeps.

3

Culm

The Culm siltstone in my father's soil is covered by rocks of the Permian and Triassic age called the New Red Sandstone and these Permo-Triassic rocks form the Redland soils of Devon. Though these rolling Redlands may now be picture-perfect, the epitome of calm and refuge for those seeking respite, their history is full of violence. Thick-bedded sandstones, siltstones and shales drowning in sea. Whole mountains that rose and fell, crumbling into water which splayed out spreads of sediment preserved as breccia rock. Then, desert. Swathes of choking heat until the mudstones of the Early Triassic, deposited in a large continental lake.

Rivers flowed in from the south, depositing gravel stones over the mudstones. Then, death. The end of much prehistoric life, as 251 million years ago, the Permian extinction – the worst in the planet's history – wiped out more than 90 per cent of all marine species and 70 per cent of land animals. Scientists estimate most species loss occurred within twenty thousand years and term the extinction 'rapid'. Twenty thousand years: rapid. To move in earth's time is to necessarily think outside the human. To learn what happens when we're not here.

Then comes a period when the earth tells us nothing. A break in the sedimentary record. In people, too, there are moments of erasure. Things buried, places that we cannot access. We may think that they look well, or just the same. But things will have disappeared; parts of them lost, or laid at the bottom of a long-forgotten sea. In time, the melting of the last ice sheets caused a rise in sea level and the lower valley of the River Exe was flooded to form the Exe estuary.

My father dreams, regularly, of the Exe bursting its banks. I am there, he says, by its side, screaming for it to stop.

'What happens next?' I ask. He doesn't reply.

The word 'culm' can refer both to this rock and to a part of a plant. The plant's culm is its stem, and in grass can grow erect or prostrate, in varying size. Usually cylindrical, they are mostly herbaceous and don't tend to last for more than a year. In rock, the word derives from coal: *col* in Old English, *culm* in Devonshire dialect. It could also relate to the Welsh word *cwlwm*, meaning knot, due to the folding of the beds in which coal is found. This rock remains for millions of years. My father's acre holds both culms, but I'm not sure about him. From what does he derive? Rock or plant? He seems so much more than animal.

'Is anyone else in the dream?' I ask. He names my brother, an old friend from Kenya, and his grandfather Frank. I wonder about the knot, or culm, of the fields in Ide where Frank used to work, the fields of the Druid. These lie further south than the Culm Measures of my father's acre and the soil there is part of the same series as the Raddon Hills that breeze in from his open window. There, the soil is loamy and gravelly, over Permian breccia and conglomerate. It tells its own story of rock falling; when the disintegrating Variscan mountains flowed down in floods during heavy rainstorms, to be deposited by the breaking water as it left its channels, fanning out its sediment. Is it such a moment that my father pictures in his dreams? Could he have a mountain's memories?

The life he had before I was born – and after, when I wasn't paying attention – felt, at first, as intangible as these falling mountains and yet there it is, buried in the soil, mine to touch and pull from the ground any time I please. And the more I talk with him of family and of fields, the more the gap closes between time and space and people. Sometimes, he dreams of vast sandscapes. Perhaps they are the Middle East, where he taught in younger days. Or perhaps they are the wind-blown desert dunes that formed the sandstones covering over the mountain sediments. Perhaps they are flashbacks to Frank's fields, where he used to walk and where I walk now, millions of years ago. Past the time of the Druids; past humans altogether; past sand, past fish, past insects, past reptiles, past plants; past ice, past sea, past sand, past rock; past erosion, past fracture, past memory, past imagining.

Do you remember a time when we were all together? I don't know if it's my father I am asking or the ground. When all earth was one continent, one landmass? The ground remembers: throwing up identical species in fossils in continents that are now large distances apart; glacial deposits of the same age and structure appearing in separate continents which would once have been joined. The Carboniferous rocks in my father's acre, under the Permo-Triassic rocks of red sandstone, remember it. They know how the last stages in the formation of the supercontinent Pangaea occurred in the Late Carboniferous period, when Western Kazakhstania collided with Baltica, closing the Ural Ocean; and the North China block collided with Siberia, closing the Proto-Tethys Ocean. Do you remember it? I ask him. How does the dream end?

He never will tell me the ending. But the ground reveals that this coming together, this supercontinent formation didn't only happen once but has been a cyclical event throughout its lifetime. I wonder if that's true of him. That he may break and that I may have to watch it. But that he'll come back together, re-form, in a deep culm of earth and time. With no end.

4

Daffodil

She cuts
She cuts light
She cuts light speech
She cuts light speech a pattered petal
She cuts light speech a pattered petalled reach.

In the week my father turns eighty, we both have the flu. Tongue is yellow, dotted red; tonsils puffed and sore. Limbs are hard to carry, the body pulling back to a standstill every chance it gets. I have been trying to decide if I'm well enough for the journey. I decide I'm not, then book the train ticket anyway. Shivering, I pack, and think about yellows.

My birthday present is going to be a list of everything yellow I see on the journey. It had started with the daffodils in the copse I picked when I last saw him. They had held the young year's rain close inside their trumpets, hoarding freshness. The same day we had squeezed lemons over pancakes for Shrove Tuesday, savouring their zest. And the broom around the garage wall had shone, and the primrose in the hedge switched on, and the undercooked apples in tight branches clung. Yellow had seemed the right colour to bring him then, and still does.

But I wonder where they should start. If it's from here, in the body, then it must be with the tongue. And the orange juice on the table, and the sun through the slats, and the Post-it note on the windowsill, and the croton leaf on the mat. Through the glass, I see it gleam. There it is on the tips of the grasses, in the one dandelion in a crack of concrete – its head laid softly on the ground, a fuzz of strength, a celebration in a cup of leaves. There are also yellow soil horizons, as iron forms small crystals in the soil. The deeper in, the yellower it can become. Mycobacterium vaccae, a genus of myco-bacteria in the soil, reduces anxiety. If I put my fingers in the soil and press and scoop, and press and scoop, could I reach it? A magic dust to hold in my palm and release into his room, a gust of calm.

It's easy, seeing a field of daffodils, to believe in colour ther-apy. To sense the power of the strident singing yellow and even to see how each of the spectrum colours might resonate their own energies. I bring him flowers. And if colour is light, of differing wavelengths, I wonder, do I bring him light?

There is always a rush to see the first flowers in the field. While the snowdrop bears the most relief after the long dark, the daffodil is the first time we dare to believe in summer, as the days fill with its quiet suns. It is thought that if you're the one in your neighbour-hood to see the first daffodil, your home will receive more gold than silver that year, and that if you take care not to step on one, you will be favoured with prosperity. A gift of daffodils is thought to bring good luck.

On the journey, this yellow vigilance helps occupy the mind. Attentive to one speck in the spectrum, I become attuned to it. In the city, yellow belongs to warnings, transport, construction. In the country: plants, birds, estate agents. As I cover the distance between us, I ask: how do you travel to another person? Physical presence gets you somewhere, but once together, verbal language can fall so short.

Combining blocks of chemicals to create new meanings, nema-todes use a chemical syntax in much the way we use words. So, as with the chemicals between worms, a quiet language of accumulat-ing repetition: there are ways of travelling without words. The soil begins to show me new ways to reach him. We will short-circuit speech through colour, gathering our yellows while we may (*Old Time is still a-flying*). I resume the vigil. Everywhere: sun. Even on a cold March day. Everywhere: light.

EIGHTY YELLOWS

for my father's eightieth birthday

All the yellows from Birmingham to Tiverton Hospital

tongue	CCTV	cloud edge	lemon
orange juice	JCB	sun dip	broom
sun through slats	high-vis jacket	office windows	daffodil
Post-it note	pay here	car light	telegraph wire
croton leaf	CCTV	alder	tractor light
grass	CCTV	poplar	daffodil
dandelion	Willmott Dixon	poplar	daffodil
bus bell	pelican crossing	forsythia	primrose
no stopping	high-vis jacket	lemon balm	sweet wrapper
neighbourhood watch	grit	lemon balm	car number plate
CCTV	security tape	mahonia	apple
Morrisons	gorse	house sparrow	pussy willow
crocus	lit larch	polyanthus	corner sign
city centre	bunting	alder	warning, forest operations
double yellow	daffodil	primrose	for sale
CCTV	straw	daffodil	danger, deep water
stay in lane	eaves	chiffchaff	laurel
HOLA! Birmingham!	pussy willow	great tit	traffic island
Spain's waiting!			
bus lane	lichen	great tit	Morrisons
JCB	max. headroom	reed warbler	sunlight

23

5

Exe

I soon reach the village and cross over the carriageway for the first time. As I walk over the bridge, a familiar feeling of nausea visits, a sick vertiginous swaying pulling me down; some old compulsion to jump. I make it, shakily, to the other side and see the brook stream out from an old stone bridge by the side of the road. My father says: *it was almost certainly after the pacification of the West by Athelstan that development of the rich land along the Alphin brook must have got under way and the bridge built over the river which Ideites used for many hundreds of years until the coming of the new link road*. Athelstan: first King of all England. I look at the now defunct bridge, over a thousand years old, and wonder that I have never noticed it before; that I have never been this side of the carriageway, despite my now frequent recent visits to the village. It reminds me just how narrow our trajectories are, even when we're actively trying to expand them.

The smell of wild garlic grows as I come closer to the river. It is a strange juncture. The brook from under the road flows into a stronger one, coming from the direction of the village. There is also a weaker brook running parallel to this, which joins up with the other. This smaller one is largely stagnant, with only a mallard moving. The brooks create a sort of island in between them, echoing an area of that name positioned further up from here, back towards the village. My father describes how *before 1841, this area, the houses making up the College and the fields at the back, was known as 'The Island'*. The area is not an island today, but quite recently, before the new road changed the environment for good, the houses

*were bound on three sides by water. Throughout the latter half of
the nineteenth century the town names 'The Island' and 'College'
are used indiscriminately in a very confusing manner.* The merged
brooks strengthen and flow under another bridge in front of the
Twisted Oak (formerly called the Bridge Inn, the *History* tells me),
a pub that I had only ever seen from a passing car, never realizing
it was so close to the village. The meeting of Fordland and Alphin
brooks seems a significant moment for some internal, bodily reason
I cannot fathom, and I feel drawn to follow this thickened water on,
on, towards Exeter; mirroring the Exe but not joining it; holding
out stoically until its final fling into Exe, canal and sea.

I have been dreaming lately, repeatedly, of the moment my father
taught me to swim. Bright orange armbands against a turquoise
swimsuit. Body as small as water is large. Arm against waist, strik-
ing out into open water. After a while, everything slackens: muscle,
limbs, thought. There is only water. Time carries me gently, until I
realize that the arm, the one keeping me safe, has gone. I turn to see
my father at the shore, and realize I have been swimming. This was
my first swim. And this flash of the north Devon coast and of childhood comes to me when I least expect it. In the middle of a city, in a
week taut with work, I wake with it fresh on my mind like shingle.

Here, though the water is not deep, there might just be enough
to swim in. It will be cold. Not summer-swimming cold; spring-
chilling cold. I will feel it in my joints which will stiffen into ice,
and the bone at the neck, my weak point, will crack. And I'll be
seen. By people crossing the bridge, on their way to the pub, or
nearby houses. But I know, even as these thoughts flow through
me, that I'll do it. I strip quickly and drop into the brook with no
thought as to how to get back out. The current is fast and strong;
I'm bent and pulled down. As my shoulders go under, cold claws
like a crow. Yet I want to go on and on, tight and light as a shard of
glass, glinting down to the beckoning Exe. As I look back towards
the island, it seems familiar yet alien all at once, as the water channels me back to another dream. This time it is the one I had in the

days before reaching the Drewshill fields, back when I could only imagine them. Then, there had been a perfect pool, and now, it is here. Only the pool is made of land, not water. The weeds are grass and the body a glass to break through. As I lift myself out, I have the uncanny sensation of having disturbed more than the water.

I dry myself with clothes I then have to wear and squelch onto a footpath that follows the brook. To my left are more fields that used to be Woolmans fields, the farm my great-grandfather Frank had worked for. I look into them, picturing him there and think of him treading this same path. What does it mean to walk where your ancestors have walked? A tall oak dominates the field. I look into its gnarled skin, the cut, marked bark; its swirling shapes hang like standing mud. It is hypnotic. Its branches reach out to me, as if to pull me back. I am walking on its very roots, some of which are raised along the path. I wonder what it can feel like to have a human walk along your roots.

That evening, the euphorbia's green pools in gold and I pick sprigs of its lit lime to take to him. I add a sprinkling of forget-me-nots that build their blue in my hand as their number increases. Since the 1940s, 97 per cent of UK wild flower meadows have been lost. The wild flowers most in danger of going extinct next are the corn buttercup, fringed gentian, yellow early marsh orchid, red hemp-nettle, shepherd's needle, corn cleavers, red helleborine, tall thrift, crested buckler fern, triangular club-rush. To name them is to remember them. By the time I reach the house, a light burst of field and sky is ready to pour from my palm into his room.

'Did you ever go swimming in the brook in Ide?' I ask him, positioning the flowers.

'No.'

'What about in any other of the rivers around?'

'No.' I think this is the end of the conversation when he adds, 'But there was the sea, of course –' A long pause drifts across the room. 'Do you remember swimming? At Instow? You went so far out, I thought I'd never catch you.'

6

Family Tree

She rings
She rings like a sweet
She rings like a sweet chestnut over
She rings like a sweet chestnut over and over bark records
She rings like a sweet chestnut over and over bark records time's
    chords.

I knew that my grandparents, Lucy and Wallace (Wally), had lived in Dunchideock and, before that, in Ide. I knew that Wally had been a farmer and butcher in Ide and that his father was called Frank and had been a farm labourer there. And I knew that Frank had married someone called Emily, though I'd not heard anything more about her. Three generations. Not a very long time for a family history to span. I think of how much further a tree would have to go back to remember its great-grandparents. A single beech might live for six hundred years, through multiple human generations. A sweet chestnut might last well over a thousand years.

'How old are you?' I ask the apple tree in the copse. 'How old are you?' I ask the white blossom. 'What do you remember?' It moves towards me in the wind. Its flower heads open and the long, slender line of the style reaches. The white stalks of filaments sway, topped with orange anthers. The moving threads look like sea creatures, strange swimming beings, tethered to their flower basin. I sense a kind of speech in them. The petals seem like hands cupped over lips that whisper.

'We remember the soil,' they seem to say. 'The sweetness in it, the cold and the warmth; we remember.' Their fluttered speech is quiet and light. 'We remember a man.' They pause, as though aware of entering rocky territory. 'The man who tended us, who moved the soil around us.'

'My father,' I breathe.

'Yes,' they say. 'We remember him. We don't see him now.'

'And what of yours?' I ask. They hesitate, moving backwards in the wind, away from me. I follow the length of their branch up to where it crosses into others, a thoroughfare of flower and intermittent sparkling leaf, catching light, aflame.

'He was here,' they say, brightening, as the sun floats through their skin, washing their white until it gleams. 'He was in the soil and in the seed.' A picture comes to me of an apple bobbing in a stream. 'He travelled here,' they say. A wasp hovers near; I am getting in the way. I mustn't hog the conversation. I press my lips to the flower tips and part; a small quiet touch at summer's start.

The copper beech is an altogether more solid prospect. The breadth of its trunk, the spread of its canopy; I am talking to an older being. I bend my ear to its burnished leaf, but colour is all I hear. A deep chestnut; a sweep of firelight.

'Who was your father?' I ask. I can barely make out the top of the tree, cannot see who I am talking to. There are parts of this tree that escape me. I look up to the plush underbelly of a collared dove. The leaves get redder the higher I look; towards the base they share more yellow and green. It couldn't possibly tell me all it has seen; this is a tree I have known, and not known, all my life.

I have started to covet the memories of these longer lived trees, to envy how in order to see the past they need only look to their own internal resources. And I have begun to picture consciousness stretched out across the centuries – mine and my father's together – and to feel how depleted it would be without my father's input. It is a recent development for me, this chestnut-envy, though I suspect it is something my father has known for some time. As a child, I recall watching him fill large sheets of paper with an evolving tree that went back centuries on my grandmother's side. And I remember that her maiden name was Archer and that this family, hundreds of years ago, was French and arrived during the Norman Conquest. That's not so bad, in chestnut terms.

But the whereabouts of this family tree now, I did not know. In the absence of the documents, I probed my father for details. It was amazing to hear that he'd had grandfathers, to place him at the age I was now, looking back across the same family. I had heard, of course, of his grandfather Frank, but grandfather William – my grandmother's father – was a new character to me. As my father recalls a poesy of primroses William brought my grandmother quite unexpectedly one day, I think of the daffodils, the euphorbia, the forget-me-nots I bring to him.

He tells me about the different families, whose name had most likely been corrupted from Burnard, and before that, from the Anglo-Saxon Beornhard. Everything he says chimes like an old chord being struck anew. He had spoken of these things before over the years but I hadn't been listening with today's attention, or with the ability to piece things together as I could now. He speaks of North Devon Burnetts, of South and West Devon Burnetts, of East Devon Burnetts and Exmoor Burnetts.

'It seems possible that the founding Beornhard was an Anglo-Saxon who came over with the army that colonized Devon under Athelstan. Don't you think?'

The question catches me off-guard. I had so far been watching this history unfold as something fully formed, simply to be received, rather than something malleable that I could, perhaps should, be helping to shape. I think about these plundering invaders: the Normans on my grandmother's side, Anglo-Saxons on my grandfather's. Each layer of settlement giving way for another, ideas of who and what is native ebbing and flowing with the years.

'We don't know, of course,' he mutters, as we are interrupted by one of the many medical matters that punctuate the days.

'Has anyone researched your side of the family?' I ask Mum. My father met my mother in Kenya in the 1960s. They married there and she came back to England with him the following year.

'Not directly,' she replies. 'But there was a cousin . . . a doctor . . . who looked into his side.'

'But the family has lived in Embu as far back as you can remember?'

'Yes, on my father's side. Mother came from Kirinyaga district.'

'Oh.' I'd always thought both grandparents were from the Kikuyu tribe, and say so.

'Yes, but there's Embu Kikuyu and Kirinyaga Kikuyu, different dialects.'

I learn that Kirinyaga refers to Mount Kenya and as British settlers couldn't pronounce it, they simply called the area Mount Kenya instead. While I read that it means 'crest of whiteness', Mum says it has more to do with godliness.

When I look in again before leaving, he is sleeping. White hair spread like a sharp frost.

7

Grass Diaries

I meet the same blade of grass in my father's acre regularly.

Twigs taper into twirls of horse chestnut. Air chokes with charcoal.

Though you are lightest, you hold the most. Water weights you in a second skin.

Dew passes, leaving you more lean. You are the length of your body, stretched out green.

You are your smell: fresh dock leaf, the pure and cleaner earth between the blades.

Birds twitter companionably around you: wrens and blackbirds, pheasant-rustles.

Cut? Found. The field is shorn but you sparkle through. I approach. First possibility that it might not be you. *It's you.*

Glittered strips of wool spun in the night. To approach means to squat, haunches wide, seeing through the strength of my legs.

Half-curve of tortoise shell with white neck: a snail folded inside you.

Transparent wings wasp over you. Pear in clover, tightly wrapped.

Beside you, last iris, head hung. Dragonfly fans its glimmering flight.

It is OK to be a bright thing in the broad earth, you say. You do not question your own presence, as I do.

Things I am learning from grass: glamour, confidence, poise, warmth.

Through a fly's wing you glow, as if through a looking glass.

Under red admiral's flight path; fur on fur; a warm flit.

Your tiny patter of breath into pear, daisy, shifting silver of birch.

Your diamond eye finds me at once, a peal of laughter in relieved air.

Today you look up to a half-moon still visible in the sun. A blackbird swoops over to urgent business in the teasel.

You are laughing, telling me a joke. Glamorous hostess of the grass, nestled in fallen oak.

End-of-day light, but your head still shines.

Pheasants in conifers ring raucous, but you hold steady, like a lighthouse, your silver beam through the blades.

You remain you, whatever is around you. You go on being you.

It takes a while for you to come. Then there are two of you, three. I have caught you entertaining. Three lights under the moon.

Only the finest cut glass, the best dinner service. You clink your bubbles.

You glint a star up from the grass, a speck of silver in the rough.

Frost holds every blade today. I must lower to see you. At ground level you signal.

You are pointing up. Up, up to the tissue of cloud and beyond to a sailing blue.

Are you still thinking of the moon?

A beech leaf by you, encrusted with sugar frost dusting its membrane.

I crane my head to hear you, 180 degrees, the sound keeps moving. *Twinkle, twinkle, little grass.*

Robin chats to chaffinch, astride the same branch. You turn to listen.

Blackbird closes in on you with urgent news, sees me and retires: it'll keep.

Tiny fresh clover just sprung from earth clumps around you. I have never seen it this small.

Today you hold a pigeon's feather, speckled in rain, carefully.

Even in dark you are light; tireless.

The air is cold around you; you nestle into blanket of beech.

A flitting to your right: a hanging leaf, catching the wind.

Ducks wheel overhead, pulling the last of your light to wing home on.

An instant hello, all spotlights turned on.

In the frozen bite of morning you are valiant and clear. *Other people will be other people*, you say. *But they can't stop you being you.*

Drizzling; pinpricks of rain on your prickled light.

Uncovered near you, an old flower marker, 'Phlox flame'. A little pocket of red.

From here, you say, *light is very near, held so skilfully in sky.*

You gleam, serene, from the mossing grass. *Don't be scared to leave*, you tell me. *All things pass.*

I wave goodbye and you push back my shoulder blades – *stand tall*, you say, *go soft and bright!*

8

Harriers

I have the advantage; his back to me as he looks across valley. As I take him in, air freshens and pulls off its skin. He turns and leaves almost simultaneously; before I quite know what I've seen, he is gone. And I think of him as a scent since that's the only way I know how to process such a thorough takeover. Lit wood and moss rising through low musk. A vapour trail over pine needles; high clouds left on low air. I don't know what I communicate, though the speed of his exit speaks its own message. Perhaps he is right to leave me. Perhaps I have not evolved well.

Another. And another. The hen harriers soar and lope in liquid loops. I move to the spot where it had been and see what it had seen: a deep dip down past bobs of sheep to Marshall's farm cupped in valley. 'Marca gesella' – 'the huts on the boundary', my father explains the name's derivation and that of the road I have come along: Markham Lane – 'marka' and 'ham' – 'boundary' and 'field or enclosure'. Drawing on N. W. Alcock's article 'Devon Farmhouses', he notes that *the peculiarly sinuous nature of the field boundaries immediately next to Marshall farmhouse may well represent the original British (Celtic) cultivation.* And the high hedges seem like curtains preserving the modesty of the curving land and for the first time I'm glad not to have properly accessed Druid's Hill; that whatever is contained in these fields is protected, that whatever it is won't be disturbed.

When I tell my father about the hen harriers he seems pleased. 'Whereabouts?'

'Pole House Lane.'

'Oh, so you've been for a walk? Good – that's where we used to walk when I was a boy. People don't walk now,' he says to himself, 'they just go to Tenerife.'

In his *History*, he mentions the Haldon Harriers as being, at one time, a local hunt. There was a *Haldon Harriers meeting at Little Johns Cross in 1864. Afterwards there was a dinner for more than a hundred yeomen and citizens of the surrounding countryside . . . The Vice-Chairman was none other than Mr Matthew Milton of Drakes Farm, Ide. To be a farmer was obviously not all hard work in the prosperous years of Mid-Victorian England!* He does not expand upon the name, though this clearly relates to the hounds and not the birds. 'These hounds,' as H. A. Bryden describes in *Hare-hunting and Harriers*, were 'big, well-boned . . . with long falling ears, drooping eyes, deep, thick hanging flews (lips), an absolute dewlap, and a most wonderful voice, deep, mellow, and, as some writer has said, possessing "the true cathedral note".'

It is an extraordinary description, to the uninitiated. I discover that a dewlap is the loose skin under the throat. That these dewlapped, loose-flewed animals should sing with a cathedral note seems fitting given the location of their hunting ground. *From the top of Pole House Lane there is not only a fine view of the Cathedral but an extensive view of the estuary of the Exe. From Celtic times onwards this must have been a fine look-out site for invaders;* church song and territorial instincts straining together for centuries in human and hound. I remember seeing the hunt a few times as a child, whirring by in its fanfare of scarlet and thudding hooves. Now the name – and the place – carry bird and hound together.

In the evening, I gather lupins in the spilling sun. A deer flanks through the apple trees. Its golden brass flares a turn, as eye to eye we dance. In the slow half-turn of a drowsy pirouette, instinct tells her to go; appled air ripens, pulling her back. As I follow her down the field, the ground has completely changed in the month since I last crossed it. High roses spill over one another, jostling

36

for the gossip of the day. Camellia leaves lie in full green. Everything is canopied, overhanging with itself. Through the tunnelled
shrubs my movements snag and tear an approach. The sound of
her bolt bursts across the wood. Fresh tracks in the mud mark her
flight over the border. Though I could get nearer, I instinctively feel
I shouldn't.

Instead, I cross the levelled-out grass of the old vegetable garden, where an army of loosestrife sing out their yellow. Streaming
with pollen, I break my way through its overpowering trails, doubling and re-doubling in the buttering flowers. The great oak sags
with low roses; dog rose floats high over crab apples. Above the
loosestrife, the field sways apricot with wheat, terracotta earth
freshly fallen from the blade. I sit with words thick and oozing.

Soon, I will take him lupins, gleaming jay-blue. But just now
I'm too heavy to move. Everywhere seems swollen and undone.
Summer casts a trance over everyone. Lupin. The word rolls lan-
guidly around my tongue. From the Latin, *lupinus*: like a wolf. It is
thought the name comes from the way it ravaged the soil, though
more recent research questions these violent tendencies. Is it true?
I want to ask the ground. Does it take too much from you? As I
eventually move off, a hawk drops, a worm lifts, and below and
above move together in a second's spark. Neither earth nor air records it. The sun leaves as usual; the grass waits for its green; birds
burrow through the darkness.

9

Indigo

Morning opens. The most delicate. The depth and the light. If you could pour softness into a flower, it would grow to this. This rooted butterfly. This in-between thing. This vegetable flower; sweet pea. Three shades mingle in petals: pink, indigo, white. I pluck the purple to take inside. A worm coils and re-coils on my calf until intercepted with a twig. Little by little we negotiate from leg to ground. Two cabbage whites spin and twist off the white sweet pea. All the day's movement is circular.

Inside, my father exercises his legs, moves them out in quick pivots. 'This is the good leg,' he says of the dexterous left that strikes out straight and true. The right crooks at the knee, but strikes out all the same. The sweet pea on the dresser pours all its depth into colour. Outside, a small snail clings to my thigh. The white sweet pea holds droplets on its pores. Next to it, a striped flying insect inserts its long body into each flower. A lilac shivers in the sudden air; a glance of rain.

More than three quarters of flying insects in German nature reserves have disappeared in the last twenty-seven years. Insect catches in southern Scotland have declined by over two thirds in recent years. I watch the sweet peas and think of all the wild flowers depending on insects for pollination; around 80 per cent of them. One disappearance triggers another. It is a strange sensation to be watching something coming to an end. How many more summers will the scene before me play out, as pollinators struggle to navigate extreme weather, the depleted flower habitats caused by intensive farming and urbanization, and harmful pesticides?

I squat on my haunches to watch the deep purple eggs hang in the light streaming through the conifers; this is the time of the plums. Steeped in a warming current of pear and peppermint they swell through the gleam of freshly rolled hay and fat buzz of dragonflies. The two cabbage whites now circle a thatch of thyme, interrupting their dance momentarily to nectar. A third joins them and their shape complexifies. One of the original two flies suddenly away, out across the fields. The other soon flies in the opposite direction, leaving only the newcomer, suckling. Two streams of air – one warm, one cool – mingle, unsure what they become when they come together. A luminous greenfly wanders over my sandy fingers. There is electricity everywhere in the grass.

My pocket hums with its clutch of orbs: the first plums, the first tomatoes. I move towards the bench but find a dragonfly already there. It makes a polite gesture of movement; I retreat, conceding it to have the prior claim. It stretches out its long torso, golden in the evening light. Basking, it glistens, resting glittering wings. In this in-between time, the air is taken over by screeching. The urgent pitching of sparrowhawks maps the fields in circles. Their rapid hawk-fire marks the air, staccatos the landscape. The cabbage whites drift around my waist, tying me with an airy bow, leaving me standing, gift-wrapped in the sun-flood. It is then my brother strides towards me through the grass, gesturing to the pile of debris he has cleared from the field, 'It's time.'

As the deep scent of smoke and petrol hits the pink notes of flowering currant and white bluebell, we sink into the ritual. Here on the hill, by the side of the fire, we throw everything in: all the anxious hours, the mourning and the dread, burn and crumble into charcoal. Our digital selves, our avatars lack this lick of fire, this all-out flame. I am glad we have come here together, stepped out of our screens, and gathered. We are only clearing the ground of its clutter, yet how better to bury emotion than to watch it fall into the earth? Even a footstep out of the fire's microcosm, the air is cold, as if the fire never was. Stepping in, the deep warm boom of being set alight. White worms of cinder snake over black grass, tangling together like fishing net. Thicker logs float fish-like over froths of ash waves, the scales of their bark glow a luminous blue. Mounds that have died down steam in peaty hills and smoke rises like a glacial landscape; all the elements are confused; none of us knows what we are doing.

For almost two hours I attend the fire. Throwing a half-burned branch deeper in, my palm covers in black chalk. Then I see her. Lazily chewing a larch leaf. She chews and watches me. This time, no immediate retreat. I back away slowly, but still she does not move. The last sun spills around her in patches, lighting the white of the clover. I turn to watch my footing as I retreat, look back, and she is gone. The deer that I have been glimpsing since the winter is starting to thaw. Each time her departure is slower. We are slowly coming to know one another, to be at ease in each other's presence, and I feel as giddy as a lover at her acceptance. Daisies glow under her hoofprints where I stand and pulse, tuning in and out. Wind ripples through the poplar. A kestrel lands on its very tip, preening its milkiness in the end-of-day light, before winging away to a further field. It is hard to switch off with so much still on. But as they retreat – deer, hawk, fire, light – so, slowly, do I.

10

July

The Hay Moon calls me from my sheets, spilling freshly over ground. The smell of pressed grass floods in from the neighbouring farm, where the field has been rolled up and left in tight bundles. Meadow grasses, red fescue, sweet vernal-grass lick along the nostrils, each with their own tang, each with their own tongue, saying something distinct about summer. I move down towards the copse when a sudden confusion of leaf, stick and hoof tells me I have disturbed the deer. I pause but don't draw back, before continuing on along the moonlight.

A rending of bark and bone cracks the air like a gunshot. I am pierced. Held to the ground by the sound. My neck snaps. Garrotted. My head hangs by a thread. I cannot withstand this battering of bodies in the trees, this frenetic beating of hearts. But just as swiftly, I snap back. If this is the time to prove I am alive, then let me look deep into its eyes. But the buck does not turn towards me. I see only the thrust of its antlers skewering the air as it moves away. I stand and listen to its sounds for as long as they come, trying to trace its tracks, to work out where it goes. I hear it burst over the hedge by the stream. I hear it thud over the neighbouring field. I hear the branches nudge back after being disturbed, the leaves return to stillness, the grass inch into its usual height.

I move along its path, fingering the places it has been: the bruised bark, the brushed flower, the silent soil. All seem full of the exchange, eager to share their side of it. The bark bears its marks on its face; the flower seeps it out through its scent; the soil recalls it passing through like a shiver. And I place my palm on the bark and feel the run of it. The blood in the antlers, the sap in the tree, the moonlight in me – running. The trill of the stream, the turn of the roots, the slap of the hooves – running. The blood in me starting to slow, soil settling below, shoulder blades finally letting go.

It is a rare sighting of the buck, as it is the doe that I know more intimately. As well as Hay Moon, the July Full Moon is sometimes called the Buck Moon in honour of the bucks' antlers coming to fullness. At this time, if the bones have not yet hardened and there is still blood flowing through the velvet membrane covering, the buck is said to be 'in velvet'. It may take a few more weeks for the bones to harden and the velvet to peel away. Until then, it will be protective of its antlers, avoiding clashes, turning away from contact. Months later, it will shed them entirely. Leave a part of itself on the ground for anyone to find, or salvage.

It was widely thought that fallow deer were introduced from the Mediterranean by the Romans in the first century AD and later brought into parks and forests for hunting by the Normans. But fossil evidence shows that they had lived here earlier, before the last Ice Age, before undergoing extinction. It is hard to think of now, this disappearance of body, when so many lives are at their peak.

Past its halfway mark, the year has let out its belt and all is expanding, all running, all roaming. In Old English, June and July were referred to as *Liða*, meaning mild, with June sometimes known as *Ærraliða*, 'before-mild', and July as *Æfteraliða*, 'after-mild'. And though the air bears a soft, scented light that steeps the velvet bone, the velvet leaf, the velvet flower, the velvet stone, there is a time after mildness, and it is coming. How long can we hold on? The mildness of moon, the bitterness of ice; the certainty of loss, the possibility of life: the deer have known it all. Each year, the antlers come and go, drop and grow in the moonlight. Sometimes the light bathes still-warm skin, a gentle rippling; other times it is a shroud, its covering: a white embalming.

II

Kulungu

She low
She lowers
She lowers her hide
She lowers her hide onto us
She lowers her hide onto us, her self into us, the whip
She lowers her hide onto us, her self into us, the whip of wind beats
  the scent
She lowers her hide onto us, her self into us, the whip of wind beats
  the scent of an
She lowers her hide onto us, her self into us, the whip of wind beats
  the scent of animal.

shhhhhhhhhhhhhhhhhhhhhhhhhhhhhhhhhhhhhhhhhhscrunchhhh   WHOSE

                    flicker. trickle. flick.   HOOVES

shhhhhhhhhhhhhhhhhhhhhhhhhhhhhhhhhhhhhhhhhhhhhh

I see nothing. By now things are starting to hurt. Wet and throbbing from uncertain paths and the tissuing light of dying battery,
the track is almost impenetrable. It is so thick with mud I keep
losing myself in its suction. I wave my wan light ahead and catch
two bright circles. Human? I shine again: two glowing orbs. Then
nothing. This show-and-tell repeats on and off for about twenty
metres. Then darkness. I can't tell if I'm hallucinating.
  Suddenly the orbs are eyes, and a body follows. A leap, a stop
and stare, another leap. Then another set of lights and a huge effort

of sinew and hide heaves across the track: two deer crossing. By now the rain is heavy and torchlight all but gone. Telling myself that it is more likely that I will get back to the house than fall forever with the drizzled deer, I keep moving. In time, a glimpse of a familiar landmark, as the rain reaches unbearable levels. But my feet have gone the other way. Back to the far wood, to the deer. I know they are there.

Ever since telling my father about the deer in the copse and his suggestion that they have come from the wood over the hill, now that hunting has stopped, I have wanted to meet them at their source; to see if there are others. I move off the track, into the trees, forward and on into the place I shouldn't be. I turn off my torch. They are moments away. I stand very still. A large tree calls; a trunk so thick it would fit ten of its neighbours. A high Scots pine, speaking. I remember Beth's advice in *The Magic Faraway Tree*, to press your left ear to its trunk if you want to really hear a tree speak. And I think of more recent bioacoustic experiments recording the sounds of the water and air moving inside them. While these are mostly ultrasonic, some sound artists and scientists have managed to alter the frequencies of the signals so they are audible to humans. These whispered clicks and silences can tell us about a tree's health, signalling, for example, when it experiences drought.

I squat beside the pine, not quite trusting the ground, and wait. The rain is so hard now, that I'm resigned to illness. I lie flat. Beneath me, pine needles break my back and collapse in the water. Hair begins to matt, rain thickens through my shoulder blades and thighs. If it ends here, what matters? Shapes seem to. The touch of leaf and wood overhead; the texture of rain which beats but doesn't break. I roll. Press an ear to the base of the tree and hear the whispered water within, and the wind's whip and the heart's beat inside the deer, inside me.

The wetness is overpowering and forces me up and back towards the path. I ache with the violence of wind. Soon it is not the wet but the cold that is keenest. In the midnight hour, the cries of the wood are deep and throated. Stars are faint and small, breathing the mineral air that is shaking; the air is shaking and the sound overwhelming. The force of the air gusting through pine, through larch, falls in swathes over the floor. As I stand in the trees, I am one. A vertical body, stretching up to sprinkled dust. My core is strong, though I freeze through each ring; each year of the body throbs with cold.

At this hour, the rain washes the smell of the earth into every crevice. Actinomycetes, with cells like bacteria and filaments like fungi, produce chemicals giving the soil this scent. There is nothing now but cold earth and wet scent. Human skin cannot handle this. Give me a hide that the rain pours off, that insulates the organs. Or let me burrow down, through the topsoil. Let it fall over me and hold while deep-rooted clover opens me to water.

I limp into the house. The wetness that gave way to cold, and the cold that gave way to numbness, is all the body is now. Slick as a slug I pour into shower and tea. Now you would think nothing of it if you saw me, a recognizable human form. The slug that slipped in from the cold; the tree that grew straight and tall in the grass; the animal that lay soft and wet in the pine, beaten by rain, flanked by trickling hooves. By the time the sun comes I have lived several different lives, yet the body holds them all still.

The bits that I left there, that sank into the soil to decompose and channel nutrients through intravenous roots, are the furthest from me now. Yet I feel them all the time. In the outward part of the skin which goes first, breaking to dust and falling to earth, there is a knowing of what is to come. In the hair that drops, in the nails that cut, there is a schooling in how to lose a body. It is the organs that resist, for the moment, that want to go on in air. But as I think back to that body in the woods, the imperceptible parts that I have left there, I feel as though something slipped. That I let go of something I shouldn't have. What is this that I am left with?

This covering of skin. Where does it begin and end? I edge towards its base: two feet that anchor. What is in them? Bone, joint, muscle? Nerves? Fat? Blood? They barely seem to belong to me.

I think of the last time I really felt them: swimming in the Alphin brook. Then, tail-like, they had propelled me, skin as scales, translucent in the water's hold. Have they been morphing since then, at some biological rate too slow for the eye, into – what? What do I need a body for now? Only to pass its nutrients on to another who needs them more. But feet are too selfish for that, too out for themselves (*stand on your own two . . .*). But I remember how they had begun to soak up water, that day at the brook. How water had turned to grass. Euphorbia and forget-me-nots into a floral sea. How each element had worked for another; and how it had all connected.

*

I don't know why we call the deer by their Swahili name (*kulungu*). Or the tawny owl that visits the apple tree (*Shamba Rafiki*: garden friend). But I think it may have something to do with friendship. Kikuyu is my mother's language, and one I never knew. But Swahili was everyone's in Kenya. I lived there for two years, while my father taught at a university. It was an easy language to pick up and always seemed to me a jolly one. Not least because the first Swahili I learned was the song '*Jambo Bwana*' ('Hello Sir!'), which was always referred to by its resounding chorus, '*Hakuna Matata*' (not the one from *The Lion King*). I heard it everywhere I went, a sort of unofficial anthem, with lyrics along the lines of: 'Hello, how are you, I am very well. Visitor, you are welcome to Kenya, no worries! Nobody worry, you're all welcome!' 'Land of Hope and Glory' it is not. And everyone is welcome in my father's acre. Since he stopped being a constant presence outside, more and more wildlife has crept through and settled. The deer use the stream at the bottom of the field for cooling off and the rhododendron bushes for

afternoon naps. Hares saunter across, happy to have found somewhere where rushing is not required. The tawny owl visits as often
as other birds let it; for its presence, if detected, gives rise to a
caterwaul of squawking, and even on some occasions, physical assaults.

But one of the first seeds for this writing came from the barn
owl. The flush of white, so much purer than any other in the landscape, came first. Then the unnatural craning of the head. *Unnatural
only to humans*, I self-correct before the word is fully out. It is the
unexpectedness – when these birds, these animals appear – that
shakes us out of our usual scripts. My father, midway through his
upstairs walk, had joined me on the landing. Minutes passed. Mini-
mal words, in whispers, though the window and several feet stood
between us and it, taking care not to frighten. We tried to establish
how long it had been there, how long we had left before it would
go. *Visitor, you are welcome, no worries!* We talked about that
owl for some time afterwards. There used to be lots, when they
first came here, my father revealed. But increased activity, from the
local farms, from us, had drawn them back. Of course, it had been
here first. We were the visitors.

Though I have lived here a lifetime, my father's claim goes back
longer, and he has an even longer claim to Ide. There he stretches
back generations, as I do, through him. But it is a mixed motion
for me. While others see him as belonging, even without knowing
his story, they do not see that in me. So while I am pulled towards
that place by all that is deeply knotted in me, I am pulled back by
those there now, who cannot see into me.

And I felt that, the last time I visited; when I wasn't recognized,
when I wasn't noticed. When I tried to speak, but was looked over, as
you do look over things that do not matter, that bear no connection
to you. Just as the bare branches of the hedge I had walked along
had given nothing away as to their species, so my skin had seemed
unfathomable. And not for the first time I had wondered when we
will be able to tell more about each other at a glance than we do now.

Perhaps as cyborgs evolve, we'll be able to download each other's information at the click of a switch, with the blink of an eye. If we could reveal our histories through our eyes, then perhaps she would have looked at me with more interest, more warmth – that woman in the village I had tried to talk to. Perhaps she would have looked at me the way my father and I had looked at that owl. *Nobody worry, you're all welcome.*

12

Layers

From the train, I see the heather's glow. Valued by Druids as a cleansing agent, many still believe in its protection. As it casts its bright beam over the land I cross, I urge it to tell me of his progress. *Is he there? Is he still there?* Ferns light up, electric; grass swims in its green; everything switching on; everywhere a heightened significance. Nearing. Our bodies beat across the fields.

This time, I find him slipped a little, yet believe he is still rooted; that the length of what is him stretches still into the horizons; that we are somehow still connected. The room fills with his steady breathing and I follow the air along its course to the open window, telephone wire and pines, out over the fields to the purple moor. There, the land is open. Is he there already? In his measured dreaming – in, out, in, out – breathing with the blackbirds.

Where does he go when he's not here? He tells me that his dreams are fast and fevered. That they take him back to Kenya, on safari, out across the bush, under the snow-capped mountain. To Oman, where we lived when I was two, golden sands stretched imperceptibly into sea. To the river Exe, plunging, churning, on the brink of some approaching catastrophe. That is where he goes when he is still mostly here. But when he slips further, where then?

As the soil sinks with a century's rain, so his bones shift; though he remains, just sunk a little lower. A buried person indicates that something has changed, that deep processes have been occurring. Beneath his acre's topsoil – silt loam – is organic matter, fine fibrous roots. Is that where he is? Beneath the organic matter, siltstone. Is that where he is? Beneath the siltstone: lime, loam, stone.

Transformation is a dominant process in the lower horizons, as clay may undergo chemical changes to its structure; or, lower down, soil may be turning from fibric to sapric as organic matter decomposes. But I do not want his transformation. I want a return, to the level days of everything knowing its place. Or can his change be so gradual that none of us notice, even him? One of those moves you look back on and see for what they were, though at the time they seemed nothing more than the natural bend of warping wood.

In this place of slippage; calcium, memories leach out. Older events stay the longest, lying more deeply ingrained, as more recent moments trickle further away. He sits quiet in the shift of natural events. Where the thick-bedded siltstone lies under water. Where mountains fell, flung and fanned into rock. Is that where he is? In the deserts? In the mudstones? In gravel? In sea?

He says *the business of a historian is not just to record what life was like in his youth, fascinating and valuable as this will always be, but to get back beyond what is there now, and beyond what is remembered by the oldest inhabitants, to what was there before that. There is no end. Always we ask the same question. What came before that?* How far back must I go to find him?

Even in the hospital, I still feel that he is here. That I just need to find the right tools to reach him. I clutch the heather in my pocket, rubbing its springing leaf between thumb and forefinger. I'm not sure what I'm releasing, what flavour of earth, flower or field, or whether hope has a fragrance. I read to him. Words spill as sounded breath to his pores, to aerate. As reading becomes a form of respiration, I scan his book for words containing 'air'. None come. I look for 'eir', and read aloud again.

SOIL MEMOIR FOR DRUID'S HILL

The first words to come, you may not hear. They may be too low or too high. Too fast or too slow. The next words will crawl underground, scraping at stone, trailing their claws along rock. Then they will be wooden, scratched in, or flapping in sap. Then they will be planted, filling with sun and sugar. The next words will be fur, damp and trammelled, riding on the back of an animal. The next words will be flutters, softly lettered beatings. It does not matter which you hear, only that you hear something. For the grass that dies back may not come again.

Horizons:
ins.
0–9
A

9–14
(B)

(B) /C The next words will worm. They'll say: The cut of the grass is not its end. The cut of the grass is not its end and the end of a leaf is a blade. The cut of the grass is not its end and the end of a leaf is a blade and the end of a blade is a sheath. The cut of the grass is not its end and the end of a leaf is a blade and the end of a blade is a sheath and the end of a sheath is a node. The cut of the grass is not its end and the end of a leaf is a blade and the end of a blade is a sheath and the end of a sheath is a node and the end of a node is a signal. The cut of the grass is not its end and the end of a leaf is a blade and the end of a blade is a sheath and the end of a sheath is a node and the end of a node is a signal and the end of a signal is a new leaf.

24+

C   It only takes one voice to bring you back.

13

Michaelmas Daisies

She remembers
She remembers our colour rise
She remembers our colour rise, in violet lace, a bride
She remembers our colour rise, in violet lace, a bride who never
  married.

shhhhhhhhhhhhhh   rushhhhhhhhhhhhhhhhhhhhrushhhhhhhhhhrushhhhh
            prrrrrrrrrrrrrrr   PIROUETTE
shhhhhhhhhhhhhhhhh~~hhhhhhhhhhhhhh~~hhhhhhhhhhhhhhhhhhhhhhh   WET   SILHOUETTE

Michaelmas daisies Havisham the lawn, stoop purple over grass, mapping everywhere with a crusting lace. Inside, my father does his morning walk. From kitchen to living room, twenty-six paces – a marathon in miniature. The scale is made to my measure, not his. His stuttering steps triple mine. Relentless, he trudges through monotonous domestic scenery. In place of elderberries, spots in the paintwork; frayed carpet for lemon balm; light bulbs for acorns. He doesn't much care to hear of the outside. I tell him about the daisies. He doesn't reply.

The first night he'd returned from hospital I'd brought flowers to his room. An hour I'd scoured the field for just the right balance of colour, memory and hope. Hydrangea, thyme and periwinkle: nothing too dark, nothing too loud. 'He won't see them.' Mum had plenty to think about besides flowers. 'His head – he can't see that high.' I'd searched for a table low enough to place them on, but soon had to make way for more practical matters: tablets and shoes; railings and frames. Little by little the house had adjusted to its owner, while the earth outside made no such allowances. For the earth has its own speed, slower than the eye. As you look at it, nothing seems to change. It has been that way always. The hills through the window. The slope of the wood, the same scattering of trees; even the sheep seem glued down.

But the landscape is a vast network of work: animal and plant, mineral and soil, and language too. The slope of the word, the same scattering of vowels, even the sense seems glued down. But it is a vast network and it is moving all the time. So that when I say 'the daisies were beautiful', I mean their shade matches the colour I brought you your first day out of hospital. You didn't see them, but I brought them. 'The daisies were beautiful' means the outside came inside to show you what you couldn't see. 'The daisies were beautiful' is running through the vase on the piano, down the walls you scrape past, nestling in the corner in the cobwebs. You don't catch it. Like a little wild thing it haunts the house, and only I can see it.

'They're on their way out,' Mum says, passing us both in the hall, 'nearly gone over.' And it's true, they are more fur than flower. 'St Michael; the day for moving,' she mutters.

'What?' I follow her into the kitchen, checked by her knowledge of English flowers. Bougainvillea, yes; coffee, yes; but daisies? 'Michaelmas, it's the day for moving.'

But the thought of coffee has pulled me back twenty-five years and I'm in Embu, in the coffee plantation, racing my cousins down to the river where the sugar cane grew. Little cousin Kinjo (actual name Njoki but she preferred it the other way around) broke it off and handed it to me. The adults used to laugh at us: me speaking only English, she only Kikuyu. It didn't matter, we always got each other's gist; lost each other in coffee found again in sugar.

'What's Kinjo doing now?' I interrupt.

'She passed away. Hadn't you heard?' Her eyes roam back over years, continents. 'That's when we thought you'd be a doctor,' she remembers, 'running around the plantation picking plants, making potions.' I return the conversation to St Michael.

'That time of year, the nuns would take us out to look at the stars.' Every sentence of my mother's is its own story.

'That's what I look forward to when I come here – seeing the stars properly.'

'You don't get stars in Birmingham?'

'You don't see them so much in cities,' I sigh – it's the same conversation we have every time I come back. 'They're much clearer here.'

She snorts. 'Kenya's the place to see the stars. The nuns taught us all their names: the Plough, the Bear . . .'

'WHAT'S THAT?' My father enters the room.

'Nothing,' she says.

'Did you see the hawk?' I ask, pulling us back to our shared territory of birds.

'WHAT'S THAT?' he repeats.

'SHE'S TALKING ABOUT THE HAWK,' Mum screams back. 'The one that comes to the lawn.'

'Oh yes. Did he say anything of interest?' he asks.

'Yes, he was asking after you,' she returns. He chuckles, shuffles back out.

This time of year I love to watch the kestrel. When leaves fall, opening the woods to the sight of its white, the sky dances with it. I follow it down from the lawn to the copse, where it wheels above the willows before winging further off. The stream below has grown heavy and sedate. It knows its own worth and strikes a lazy pose on the land. The urge to be in it is immense. I fling myself downhill before I can convince myself not to. Up close the water is quick and brown. What looked easy from above is urgent at the root. It rushes down, gathering earth pigments, rocketing over rock in a rush of mud, a swirling dirty foam. It is murky and bleak and all desire to be in it is gone. But as I brace myself for the long ascent back, something catches me in the tight corner of an eye. A flash of white and a turn. I rotate towards it and find a feather breaking the surface. It rises like a dancer in a musical box, its circuit perfectly poised. Time slows and the movement seems to gather everything in; leaves and tongues soak through it, memory too.

He came down wrong and something snapped. Came out of its socket. Crunched the bone where he hung. The kestrel that fell and lay there for days, feathers splayed at sickening angles.

He keeps falling. Slowly gains momentum to move again, little by little, edging out. How many wounds the body takes, how many violences. And it heals. And it heals.

14

Nutrients

shhhhhhhhhhhhhhhhhhhhhhhhhhhhhhhhhhhhhhhhhhhhhhhhhhhhhhhhhhhh
fluff. glove. stroke. (seep. tseep.) pour. PURR EYES SURPRISE
purrrrrrrrrrrrrrrrrrrrrrrrshhhhhhhhhhhhhhhhhhhhhhhhpurrrrrrrrrrshhhhhhhhhh

'What is an ecopoet?' he asks.

'Well, they write about the environment but . . . perhaps from the perspective of highlighting its issues and wanting to help . . . maybe with activism,' I stutter.

'But what's your activism? You haven't done anything!' My father sums up the angst of every environmental writer in two sentences.

'Well, you can lobby your MP, you can support charities; it could even just be the choices you make with products, you know, decisions you make on a daily basis.'

'What's the most harmful product for the environment?'

I've really just looked in to see how he's doing and was not expecting *Question Time*. 'Well, we need to be careful of anything adding carbon dioxide right now, contributing to climate change.' *Please don't ask me anything about climate change.*

'Oh.'

I skulk back out.

The wood is showing signs of a big night out: upturned apples strewn like beer cans, magpies, pigeons whose hair has fallen out, leaving fluffy little Mohawks in the grass. Late revellers lie back in the branches, resentful at my disturbance, poke faces around branches; hop closer than usual – heads too full of sleep to quite

57

make me out. A feathered face plays Peepo: branch left; branch right; thinks me a hallucination. It chuckles to itself with a tic-tic-tic before heading back to bed. It has a face you would never tire of stroking. Wooded velvet.

Today I bring him roses. The subtle climbing dog rose and the Wild Rover rose's loud flare of wellness, of triumph against the dark. The Rover has a scent so intense you cannot run from it. There is no hiding from its blast of health. Fresh from the raspberries and the deer sidling past it on its way to cool by the stream, oak leaves in its fur, lemon mint through its hooves. The rose is picked from the dew that pools above this, that drips onto the nettles, through the long grass that catches it in cobwebs. This I bring to him, and leave in the side of the room, where he will not see but absorb it. It sits there like a toast: to the purpled red days in the veins, pumping flaring jumping.

I crave one more burst before returning to the city, one more touch. Returning to the wood, I press my middle fingers to the ground, leaving little skinprints. In the soil-space of these fingerprints live up to a billion bacteria. The figure is almost unfathomable, like light years, or global debt. There are 7 billion humans over the earth, but a billion bacteria every few centimetres under it. If it ever comes to a mutiny, I don't fancy our chances. Yet far from ousting us, these hidden helpers work to our advantage, converting the air's nitrogen into forms that plants can use. They feed the plants who feed us. Through the soil we gain the nitrogen that gives us protein, potassium that aids our muscles and circulation, calcium for our teeth and bones, magnesium for our heart, phosphorus for our brains and nerves, sulphur for protein and growth. And how can we feed it? While chemical fertilizers may provide nutrients to plants, they don't replace other kinds of food that the bacteria and fungi in the soil need.

Farmers can help the micro-organisms in the soil, as they help us – through mulching, using cover crops and no-till farming practices. Here, in the field, we've used our own mulch, grown our own vegetables, fruit, flowers, trees. But I can't remember doing much in the years I lived in gardenless flats in London. Now, in Birmingham, although there's a garden, as a rented property I don't have free rein over it. I wonder what the figures are on this; people disconnected from the soil because of lives too transient to grow attached to it.

As I let the soil sprinkle through my fingers, I long to be able to transport its calcium up the field to my father, its phosphorus along skin to my own nerve endings. I think of his question of how to help the environment and of the carbon present in my answer. The soil holds around twice the amount of carbon found in the atmosphere and in plants. Storing it here reduces the amount present in the atmosphere and is the basis of soil fertility, releasing nutrients for plant growth and filtering harmful substances. The red dust speckling my capillaries, glowing brightly in the cold, means so much to me and yet, I wonder how I can care so much for one patch but so little for another. My Birmingham land stings with neglect, like a friend I have been too busy to call. For however long it is mine to move over, there are still billions of lives inside it, relying on me for succour, as I rely on them. A spoonful of soil holds more organisms than there are people on the planet. How many more still in the disused, untended plots around the city. I think about urban farms, cropping up wherever there are cracks; about seasonality and the month that I am in. And as I smooth the last touches of soil from my skin, I think once more of my grandfather and his favourite vegetable, which also happens to be mine.

'When's a good time to plant broad beans?' I ask my father, as I look in to say goodbye.

'October.'

'Do you mind if I borrow a trowel?'

15

Osteoporosis

She scurries
She scurries as a spider light
She scurries as a spider light and care
She scurries as a spider light and care full.

She hears
She hears our language
She hears our language secrete
She hears our language secrete under her feet a secret
She hears our language secrete under her feet a secret sequence.

My hand reaches to steady the rest of me and lands on an apple tree, completely laden. I stop short, extend arms to branches: an apple midwife. Spotted with autumn, their ripeness is in the touch; small tugs on the waist, fingers around the spine. Cradle their ribs. Exert just enough pressure. Sometimes, two come at once: a twin birth. Other times, ones that look ready aren't; you have to listen to the tree, you have to go on touch. Blackberries bleeding overhead, apple mushing underfoot; acorns: little spits of light in the dark leaves as I pick. These globes glow in the hand: the traffic lights of changing seasons. Green to yellow to red, they pulse and pause in my upturned palm. 'Not yet,' lisp the younger ones, clinging with all they've got. Others, drowsy from the sleep of the seasons, sigh: 'Is it time?' Whole summers asleep in the flesh; a crisp wintering of skin.

Pockets weighted with apples, I strike out across the field. The throb of me pushes all sound down a syphon; vast at the top – the wide blast of road traffic; minute at the tail – pinpricks of insects clicking on and off in the grass. 'Fartlek', a deliciously stupid word, has always been part of my running arsenal, long before I knew it had a name, or was a verified practice. Mostly when I start to get bored, or the body starts to hurt, I spurt into a shock sprint which lasts for as long as the terrain of ground–body allows. There is a joy in speed, an absolute letting go of the mind, similar to the first onslaught of the cold in outdoor swimming.

What is underfoot dictates the speed of the run. A clear path quickens; long tundra, potholes, the untilled meadow slow and stall. There are other slowing factors: a plastic hawk the farmer next door uses to ward off birds; the real hawks that attack it; the bitter screech of a chainsaw. As I run, I am conscious of not speaking the language, of the weight I give the grass and the ground below, the pressure on the soil. The millions of hectares abandoned every year to erosion. To which I add the weight of the ribs, the pulse of the head, the thundering heart. I don't even know who I'm not speaking to. What is grass? What is in and under it?

There are over eleven thousand species of grass. And it is really a canopy of leaves. At least the top part, that grows out of the stem and most often meets the human eye, is leaf. Their fibrous roots stretch into the soil, drawing up water and nutrients, sometimes spreading out to grow new plants, tethering grass to ground. Often, a ligule covers the lower part of the leaf: a thin membrane or fringe of hair-like strands. As I run, I tread the leaves' hair, catching light. They photosynthesize, like those of a tree. I run green.

My father has always run. In his youth, for the local running club; then at university; and in later life competing in hundreds of marathons. Navigating the country lanes daily by foot, the earth for miles around our home has been imprinted by thousands of his steps, the ground pushing up to meet him; his soles, the portals through which the underworld could travel. I feel this as I move over his old ground. Feel this underground movement, tiny tremors through the clay to leaf litter and humus, down to trickling roots and minerals, to sand and silt, to iron and aluminium oxide, to bedrock. And all the way back up. If there is speech in this, it is in the movement, in the drift of chemicals and their re-settlement.

In the chemical language of nematodes, adding one more chemical to the signal for 'go away' means 'come here', perhaps showing that, for worms too, there is a fine line between love and hate. Like the control of traffic at Birmingham's Spaghetti Junction, worm thoroughfares throb with held and repelled worm traffic. I think of Druid's Hill and the 'sinuous' field boundaries of Alcock's description. We read these curves now as signals of the former Celtic cultivation; will future readers see the road's curves as our own method of working the land?

Soon, lane becomes road, and a slope down along steeply falling hill. I gust in huge lungfuls; golden leaves canopy over and sun trickles lightly through as I run. Not for the first time, I think of how my travels into the soil, the past, my father's imprints, are opening up new kinds of living to me, are making me live a wider life. I reach the road that he would call 'the lung opener' when we'd walked it together. It takes a while to scale and my speed decreases practically to walking pace, but eventually I make it. As the road flattens out, I move with speed, though I am making the same amount of effort. It seems the perfect metaphor for privilege.

I reach Arthur's wood, where it feels good to swap tarmac for earth, moss, pine needles, to slip my way through the red sludge, adding my print to the paw and boot marks already there. Rain pulls a deep cloud over and it is suddenly dark. Trunks rise high, pointing up towards the source. A blackbird flits between the pines like a bat. The rattle of haulage trucks seems about to burst through the trees, though it is only coming from the road. That such an open, public wooded space exists so close to the village feels special. Coming out against road again, I see a 'For Sale' sign on the gate. I wonder if it includes any part of the woodland that has always, in my living memory, been a communal space and feel suddenly self-conscious and in the wrong place.

I move back through the woodland, surreptitiously, not along a path but through the low-branched trees. I have to bend low to pass through them and feel my stomach muscles draw in at the challenge. I probably shouldn't be here, but the sign's threat of the land being taken away propels me into rebellion. I slink along the forest floor, all animal. The going is soft; here and there a needle pricks into skin. I make a mental note to remove them before rejoining the public road, along with the powdered pollen on my legs. A moth flutters by my fingers; we all match perfectly and seem synecdoches of each other: the dusky drab looper moth, my tawny hand, the rose-brown pine-needle floor. As I continue at ground level, I see seedlings shooting up, husks of pine cones and endless carcasses of out-grown, or burgled, shells. There are nests too, fairly low in the branches, so that you can see their spiralling patterns of twig. Nearby are quite large white wood pigeons' eggs, broken open. Elsewhere along the floor are golden tissues of leaves, paper thin. Their gold gleams against the soft green moss. I want to pick it all up and carry it back with me to lay as my floor in Birmingham, in place of MDF.

As I rejoin the road, homeward bound, I start using the whole space, veering into the middle when there's no one else around. I run along a brook, back into banks of gleaming foliage, and brace myself for the long ascent. I wonder if this is how he felt, on every return from wherever he'd run; living at the top of a hill, the return is always going to be an upward challenge. But instead of the slow chug of my earlier climb, I find the body gliding into gear, some old chemical reaction pulsing through the body, something imprinted in the hormones or entangled in the DNA sending me flying uphill. Finish strong, some implanted voice is saying. And I do. As I burn over the brow, the road parts into a sea of onlookers – who happen to be clouds, meshing into panoramic green. I pull into the lane, singing with green and gold and airy applause.

Even in the moments where nothing moves – not chemicals, not words, not bones – there can be a silent progress under the surface, can't there? A healing? I think of that, as I retrace the soles of his feet, covering the ground that they covered. Mountain ash clutches heat in its leaves. I grasp it as I go; a handful of heat to take in to him. Pollen falls. Web trails. The grass is a network of diamonds. Can't get a word in. Grass interrupts. Incessant. Do I know what it's like to have a diamond for a head? To carry a circle of light? To be colour? In place of bone to have lignin, cells and fibres? Carbon and oxygen; nitrogen, phosphorus; chlorophyll, cellulose; water and green? Its chatter is fast and light and linked. It chimes with the other blades – clover, a dock leaf, a fallen apple, a tangle of roots – endlessly signalling, twinkling, tinkling, and always looking up. Do I know what it is to be always looking up? To pine cone, needles, passing cloud and blue?

Inside, my father looks down, curved by brittleness of bone. Inside, the house is full of spiders, escaping the farmer's harvest blade. They scatter over draining boards, the back of the sofa, windowsills, on their way I don't know where. I don't want to move them. I love the multiplicity of leg. Two is too limiting. Two stalks of bone that break apart with the movement of months. That wear down, into smaller and smaller steps. That can't take you anywhere anymore; that leave you relentlessly inside your own body, with nowhere left to run.

16

Protozoa

She springs
She springs and prances as she dances
She springs and prances as she dances with the stars, the soil her sky.

I sense movement below. No scurrying of foot or flapping of wing. Something is tumbling. I drop my head low, I tense my toes; far beneath them something flows. In the top six inches of the soil, aquatic animals called protozoa entrance me. Single-celled animals living in a film of water surrounding soil particles. A hidden water life in the soil. As a wild swimmer, I am enthralled, not only by the proximity of this secret water life but by the very notion of aquatic animals: a contradiction in terms for the land-locked.

Their name, 'proto' 'zoa' means first animals, with a freshwater species called 'heliozoa' or 'sun-animalcules'. The names are intoxicating. When I enter a river there are three stages: 1) the plunge: complete denial of water temperature as body enters before mind can stop it; 2) the shake: vigorous movement to raise body temperature which lasts for as long as it takes for the pain to subside, generously termed by others as 'swimming'; 3) the float: lying still, on the back, face up to sun, cloud, rain- or snow-fall. During the float I am heliozoa: one of the first aquatic animals staring at the sun. In these moments, colours intensify so as to become meaningless. Or, they no longer match their meanings, as if an OuLiPo poet had performed a language constraint on them, taking the word 'sun' and moving to the entry nine times below it in the dictionary and attaching that word's meaning instead. 'Sun: a small brightly coloured bird of warmer parts of the Old World, resembling a hummingbird but not able to hover.' In these moments, you know what it is to be light. To not be pushing down on the earth, not lending your weight to what is already laden.

Of the groups of protozoa, one is the amoeba, and of these, an actinopod amoeba is shaped like a star. As I run, I start sculpting my own body accordingly, throwing out my arms as my legs jump apart. I realize I am doing star jumps. As I run, I start to feel the stars jump beneath my feet and to match them. I feel them through the soles of my shoes, their vibrations meet mine in the twined nerve endings of toe and soil. Lightness is both a colour and a weight. Stars are animals. The soil needs its own dictionary.

Protozoa: animal stars under the earth, consuming bacteria, releasing nitrogen. Fungi: threads of nutrient cycling, binding soil particles together. Humates: the concentrated nutrients and complex compounds from the breakdown of animal and plant life over millions of years. Nematodes, earthworms and arthropods; molluscs and grass; all breathing all moving all chattering in their own processes for breathing, for moving, for chattering. Cherts, lavas and tuffs. Breccias and sands. Mudstones and flint and ice and silt. Carboniferous, Devonian, Permian, Triassic. Cretaceous, Palaeogene, Quaternary, Drift. I don't yet have all the names for all the processes. I have to keep looking them up and to keep looking down.

17

Quarter

She uses words
She uses words to help us stop
She uses words to help us stop falling
She uses words to help us stop falling but what do words add
She uses words to help us stop falling but what do words add up to?

A quarter of all known species live in the soil. Bacteria, fungi, plants, organic matter, nematodes, arthropods, animals. Some single-celled bacteria, some with billions of bacteria in a single gram of soil. Some decomposer bacteria, breaking down organic materials; some nitrogen-fixing bacteria, converting nitrogen into forms that plants can use. Some disease-suppressing bacteria; some actinobacteria, breaking down humates. Some sulphur oxidizers, converting sulphides into plant-friendly forms. Still more aerobes and anaerobes, adapting to the oxygen levels in different kinds of soils. Fungi decomposers, breaking down organic matter. Mutualists, like mycorrhizal fungi, developing mutually beneficial relationships with plants. Soil is one of the most complex ecosystems we know, or don't know. There is still so much to find out.

The statistics in our reading of the soil can feel too large to comprehend. There are 270 million dairy cows currently being farmed worldwide. These dairy cows and their manure have a direct impact on the soil. Not only do they add large amounts of greenhouse gases – methane, nitrous oxide and carbon dioxide – into the atmosphere, contributing to climate change, but overgrazing and the impact of cattle movement on the soil can lead to erosion, with the loss of topsoil and organic matter that can take centuries to grow. 270 million cows. 66 million people in the UK. 7 billion people in the world. One dairy cow to every twenty-six people in the world.

Catering for this high volume of one species can also see a reduction in others, as natural habitat is converted into agricultural land in order to produce feed crops for cattle or provide pasture. Subject to their own particular gentrification, the less tangibly valuable species move further out, even as the areas left to host them diminish. I think of the teeming bacteria in the soil, how these populations work for the good of so many, against the limited roles assumed by humans. Sometimes saviours: saving our soil, our water, our planet; other times, villains: we created our own crises. We lurch from hero to demon, often overlooking the value in the small everyday consciousness of being neighbourly.

Noticing, with friendliness, what is around, or not around, us. Not stopping at the limits of our knowledge but pressing on and in and on and in, gently, tentatively, politely. Farmers, with their daily contact with the fields and their occupants, have pioneered innovations that are making dairy farming more sustainable. Many know that keeping a closer eye on the cows can contribute towards reduced disease and increased milk yields, but a friendly noticing prompted one farmer in Sweden to prepare quality rubber mattresses for her cows to sleep on. Their improved welfare, also helped by new housing, led to saved costs in other areas. Since the cows no longer need so much professional attention, she says she is able to spend more time with them companionably. 'Now I have more time to just be around them,' she says.

What do I notice in my visits to the fields? In the time spent with the blade of grass in my father's acre? That I am often the beneficiary of these moments. The fields, in ways I am only just beginning to realize, connect me to my father, while the blade of grass leaves me, somehow, more graceful, more upright. While all I do is write of them. Yet there may be a value in this amplification, in the bringing of these characters into the foreground, in changing the way they are looked, or not looked, at. And this *not looking* is one of the hardest things to visualize, to make it possible to see.

A quarter is a statistic that is more readily realized. To know that a quarter of all known species live in the soil is to picture a packed thoroughfare, a burgeoning network of interlaced lives. But knowing that a quarter of all soil is severely degraded is less easy to see. Perhaps we envisage eroded soil in distant continents where plants cannot grow. Perhaps we see floods, where degraded land is unable to hold onto water. Or perhaps we can't picture it at all.

While there is still so much to learn about the soil, we know that the interaction of organisms in the soil contributes to the cycles that make all life possible, and that to help ourselves we must help the soil. Whether it is a story that shows us that, or the maths, what matters is that we see it.

18

Ritual

Just as a bird feels the moment to fly, to set off across country, continents, to new ground, I feel the time when I must leave what I am
doing and come. And each time I visit the Druid's Hills, a force rises
from the ground to meet me. While logically it seems futile, this
regular touching of a particular piece of land, I continue, following
an inner knowing that won't explain itself. I wonder about these
internal rhythms, guided, perhaps, by a flow of external currents:
the length of day, or temperature.

For me, they are currents tied to my father's condition. The fields
call when he does. Yet, because he must be well enough for me not
to need to be with him while I come to them, they also hold a sense
of hope. They are a place not of climax or collapse but of holding
on. And I offer them up to him, differently, each time. Sometimes
it is the approach to the fields that draws him – as I tell him of my
walks on paths that he walked as a boy, or of passing close by sites
that he has featured in his research. Other times, it is the family
connection to the fields: what kind of work great-grandfather Frank
might have done there; whether great great-grandfather James
may have crossed them. Occasionally, it is the fields themselves:
what wild flowers are scenting, what animals grazing, what grasses
growing. There is always something that sparks a flicker of interest
that brings him back to the living moment.

And they fascinate me too, though I didn't know them as a
child. My childhood attachment is to my father's own acre, so that
his field and the Druid's Hills fuse together in my belonging. It is
also something to do with words, this external current that draws

me and draws him; an etymological mining, uncovering the past. How we see the Druid in Drewshill; how we glimpse the burial mound, *crich*, in Churchills field. And we both sense the import- ance of this looking, this tracing of the debris of words left in language. What will happen to these words if we don't look closely enough at them? Where will they go?

So while I cannot adequately explain to others why I travel a hun- dred and seventy miles, drop to my knees and use my hands to touch this soil, I know that it is all these things: a chill in the air, a call from a father, a grandfather, a grass, a flick, a kick, an ember of a word, things vanishing calling out to be heard. And there is a hearing, too, in touch. As birds combine multiple senses to navigate, so do I.

Birds can get compass information from the sun, the stars, from landmarks, and some, like homing pigeons, can smell their way. They can also sense the earth's magnetic field, through methods that have long been debated. Recent research indicates the possibil- ity of a protein in birds' eyes that is able to detect magnetic fields, allowing the birds to navigate through a sense called magneto- reception. For me, this sense is in the fingertips as well as the eyes. As I brush the soil I am called to, I travel deeply into the earth's fields, its tremors and ripples; notes, trills, trickles.

And as I dig, the soil sears pink like a perfect steak. I scoop it into my palm, rolling like dough. Parts are gritty, sand grain par- ticles not yet broken down. And the grass bends with the weight of its task, breaking down the bedrock as its roots join forces with fungi, dissolving minerals. I feel this too: the grass rooting in the soil; the trees' deeper tracts tunnelling from the hedge. And I feel the moment that the ancestors of these plants arrived, perhaps 400–350 million years ago in the Devonian period, pulling up from water to land. The force of the water at the root of everything, the call from the brook at the foot of the field, from the river it will meet, from sea. I feel the water even as my feet fix fast in the earth.

It is in this period, named after the county of these fields, that soil, the kind of soil we know now, evolved. When these early land-dwelling plants put down first roots; when larger trees tunnelled further; when deep rooting systems spread beneath the ground. The higher temperatures saw greater oxidation in the rocks, intensifying the red pigment, leaving the red rocks we see today. Then, as plants spread and the carbon dioxide in the atmosphere reduced, the climate changed, becoming more like what we know now. And now that it is changing again, I want to ask the soil what will happen. Will plants rescue us or give us up as lost?

None of this now concerns great-grandfather Frank, whose own touch on this land left years ago. Nor, I imagine, do I, born years after his death. And yet there is something about his having been here, some imprint that bonds me to this field. And it matters that Grandfather Wally worked the land around here too. And it matters that my father walked through it, and in his childhood lent a farming hand.

When the Anglo-Saxons gained Devon's Redland soils as the spoils of battle, they pushed the native Celtic farmers uphill, further from the riverbanks. The Druid fields lie between the plush soil along the Alphin brook and the high footholds of the Haldon Hills. Although this soil is still sought after, farming here has always had its challenges. My father chronicles how the fortunes of the local farms waxed and waned between the nineteenth century and the First World War, noting the lasting impact of the Hungry Forties. In the present moment there is uncertainty over changes to farmers' subsidies. For decades, UK farmers received substantial EU subsidies, and while the shortfall is being covered in the short term, the longer view is unclear.

In its very material way, farming brings together the local and global. An unfavourable weather event in one part of the world may create demand for produce in another. A political decision in one country may affect trade in many. Customer demand in distant lands can dictate the growth of each tiny life within a local field. Time ripples and echoes through these issues as my father, writing of the 'new' agricultural crisis in the late nineteenth century describes how *the exploitation of the American prairies, the intro-duction of fast, refrigerated ships and the import of meat from South America and New Zealand meant that the worst fears of those who had argued against free trade some fifty years before were realized; the British farmer now had no defence against the importation of cheap corn from abroad.* For centuries, the other-than-human lives in the fields have been connected to, and reliant on, events far from their locality – and the human lives bound up with these fields have been intrinsically affected.

After moving from Ide and the Woolmans fields, my grandfather settled closer to the Haldon Hills, in Dunchideock. This place of my father's later childhood used to have farmland: cows that my grandfather would milk, and milk that my grandmother would turn to butter. Now, though there is no farming, it is still a fam-ily home, a pocket of a British settlement, surviving in the Haldon Hills. As I stand in the Druid's fields, I point one arm towards Haldon, the other back towards the Raddon Hills where my father is now, body prising out like a compass.

All the skin of me, the pigment, the falling dust, is called to the soil. All the water of me, the churning motion, is called to the fish: the bony lobe-fins, ancestors of dinosaurs and mammals, whose fossils remain in the Devon rocks. All the heart of me, the puls-ing inside, is called to the pulsing outside: the grass, the birds, the insects, the worms; and further, to the beating that continues beyond the earth, beyond anything tangible: to my father's fathers. And him, on the border; a branch held out to me, as a root slips back to his fathers.

It is all this I wonder about, as I process the pull that takes me from my seat, my desk, at a table, in a room, in a building, in a city, miles away. And wonder, here, assumes all its awestruck resi-due, all its retinue of surprise. So that thinking and feeling and not knowing are held together in the same space, silently filling the body with a growing pressure.

19

Stars

The farm I'm visiting, on the eastern fringe of Dartmoor, came into the family at the start of the twentieth century. Before that, it had been part of the extensive Gregory estate. When I arrive, I'm shown a picture of this paternal founder, an imposing man with a prominent dark moustache, proudly holding a sheep. Since its early days in the family – John, the present farmer, tells me – the farm has grown from 150 acres to around 450.

'What kind of a farm is it?' I ask, self-conscious about knowing so little.

'Beef and sheep,' John says.

'Any crops?' I ask.

'Some kale and corn to feed the animals through the winter.'

'And what kind of soil is it?'

Here everyone speaks at once. 'Sandy,' says John. 'Silt,' says his son. 'Granite,' says the other son.

'A kind of sandy granite,' John concludes.

I'm pleased to find them as interested as I am in this living land that most of us move over without thought. And of course the farmers have the closest contact, the bodily knowledge as well as the scientific. I see the rich dark grain beneath his fingernails.

'How do you find it?' I ask, 'Is it all right for the crops?'

'Well, it's high up. It's not very deep, not as good as clay – nothing like the kind round you.'

'The Redland,' I say.

'Oh yes, nothing like that. I suppose they grow a lot of corn around you? John asks, wistfully.

'Yes, pretty much all around,' I confirm. 'But you do OK with your soil?' I press.

'Oh yes, we do all right. It's hard work, but I've done it all my life, you know.'

'What's the hardest part of the job?' I ask. Once more, they all talk at once. Paperwork, hedge-trimming when harassed by impatient drivers, lambing, calving, ploughing. But the paperwork gets the longest attention.

'We've got to go online now,' says John's wife, with a shudder. She has been the bookkeeper for the farm, as has often been the way with the wives. 'Soon it will all have to be online.'

'Will that be difficult?' I ask.

'Oh yes, a lot of these farmers don't use computers, you know. I don't know what's going to happen.' It's a phrase that recurs often through our conversation. I don't know what's going to happen.

'All the cows have passports,' one of the sons interjects. A collective eyebrow is raised.

'Passports?' I repeat.

'Yes, I'll show you if you like.' He comes back with two kinds of cow passport, an older kind and the most recent. Each animal has its own document, complete with barcode. I start to understand the scale of the paperwork. We laugh about it, but it's a dark humour, the kind only possible in adversity.

'And is the farm doing OK at the moment?' I ask.

'The price of lambs is down a bit – it goes up and down – it all depends on what the supermarkets want,' one son says.

'A lot of people are vegetarian now,' I observe. 'There's a growing call for that, environmentally. What do you make of that?'

'It's up to them, isn't it?' he shrugs. 'People can do what they want.'

'But what will they eat?' John demands. 'What will we feed people on?' Some speculation follows about different food sources. 'Well then, how will they keep the forests down,' John persists, 'without the animals grazing?' It is interesting to listen to this conversation between generations: John in his eighties, and his sons, continuing into a very different world.

'What are the plans for the farm,' I ask, 'will it carry on in the family?'

I don't know what's going to happen, their faces say.

'It may go to the niece and nephew,' one of the sons ventures.

'Is anyone else in the family still farming?' I ask John. He names three other farms, including one in Christow, where I knew my grandmother had come from but I now had no personal connection to. The sense of things coming to an end is pervasive; a whole way of life obscured, as if by snow – adrift.

'What are the best parts of working on the farm?' I continue.

'Harvest,' they all chime. 'It's hard work, but if the weather's good, it makes all the difference. Silage's not a bad job.'

'We had an early spring,' his wife says, and I think about the environmental changes that may have brought this. 'And dry. So harvest started well. But after that, it got worse and worse.'

'The bluebells,' John says. Everyone smiles. 'And here, you can get on the hills and see for miles. With flat land, it may be easier, but you've not got the views,' he continues. 'Here, it's hard work, but I've done it all my life, I'm used to it. And father used to do it, with horses.'

'There's Hingston Rock, that borders our land,' says his wife, as the panoramas come to life around them. 'Even better's Blackingstone.'

'Oh yes, you get to Blackingstone,' John agrees, already there in his mind. 'On a clear, dry day you can see Torquay. On a clear, dry day, you see it all.'

That night, there is a full moon, a super moon. So far, I have witnessed all the year's lunar events in Birmingham, where light pollution saps the brightness (or, as Mum would put it, *Don't you get moons in Birmingham?*) but tonight, I'm in Devon. Leaving John's farm, darkness thick as rock, we crawl our way back to the house, careful of what we cannot see. I go to bed, but can't settle knowing it's out there: the great white pulsing. I don't want to wake the house but know I must go. Pulling on socks and coat over pyjamas, I pad down the stairs.

As I open the door, the moon has a bewitching quality, quite unlike the sun. Its light is less airy, more liquid. A falling star shoots down, a rush of white against the gloom. In the instant I see it, I send a wish for his health; even before I fully realize what it is, I have wished. How ingrained upon us that superstition must be, as quick as fight or flight; fall and wish. The cloud is fast-moving in front of the moon. My father coughs and mutters to himself; I can't tell if he's awake or asleep. As I pull the door shut, another shooting star falls, high over the pear tree. Clouds shift fast beneath the stars, keeping everything moving.

I stand out in the wide night. An owl hoots from further down the field. The grey cloud moves under the moon like smoke from a fire. When it clears, the brilliance is intense. It is like nothing else. As I gaze up, I see three stars in a row on a diagonal under it: Orion's Belt. I wonder if I'm seeing any planets.

I take slow, deep inhales, eyes closed; exhaling into moon. As they open, my eyes fill with whiteness; I blink in the showering stars, pull eyelids over constellations. I want to move towards the moon but the loud cacophony of pheasants departing trees as I approach prevents me. My heart rackets out of my ribs as I walk into a tree just as a pheasant is exiting. The breeze is gentle and unseasonably warm. Moon laps like milk over my skin and I sink back into its softness: Cleopatra of the moonlight.

This is the Geminids' meteor shower. The meteors have been predicted without enthusiasm by astronomers, since it was thought the full moon would make it too light to see them. Slower moving than most meteors, these are, unusually, formed from the debris of an asteroid rather than a comet. Though the December full moon, also known as the Oak Moon, Cold Moon or Long Nights Moon, is brightly out, the meteors are visible here. The December moon always shines near the stars of Taurus, the stars of my birth, and it glitters like a birthday present.

Tonight is the only night in the month when the moon will stay in the sky all night long. I stay out as long as the raucous pheasants and the worry of disturbing those inside the house will let me. At the precise moment that the moon is at its fullest, I retreat, leaving behind me a new influx of owl song, a faint fluted rippling. To fall asleep watching a meteor shower is to feel the lids sink and vision blur, only that blur is not sleep but speed: the swift shimmering of an asteroid. It is to adjust the eyes to motion and the heart to joy. Sudden sparks dismantle me, leaving only the good parts. I fall and sleep and wish in the silvering.

20

Teign Valley

'All right if I look around?' I ask the man shuffling around one of the many disused railway carriages.

'Go ahead.' He looks me up and down. 'You're not interested in railways, surely?' Once more, as with the Ide villager who could not picture my relation to the place, I long for a cyborg attachment making external form match internal.

'More interested in the area,' I concede. 'My grandmother was from Christow.' He brightens.

'Oh really, when would that have been?'

'Well, she was born in 1911.'

'The railway would certainly have been here then,' he chuckles. I think we are about to settle into a nice nostalgic reverie over what the railway would have been like then, but instead he asks, 'Would she have taken the train?' I have no idea.

'Oh, possibly,' I hazard.

'It's amazing how people take their cars now, for distances people would think nothing of walking before. A couple of miles. What's a couple of miles over a hill? It's all cars now.'

Should I tell him that I walked a couple of miles to get here, that I don't own a car? I think better of interrupting his flow. He looks fondly at a picture of the railway from the 1950s and points to the station building.

'This is what I'm rebuilding now. Just this building and these water carriers here, where the water would be used to . . .'

I nod appreciatively but cannot remotely picture these mechanics. He shows me the map of where the railway used to run and all the parts that have now gone. He enthuses about the recently reopened track in Scotland. I've heard about this and say so; he reports how it's been so successful they're looking to extend the line now.

'If they can do it there using our money, well . . .' It's only then that I realize he plans to reopen the Teign Valley railway line.

'Are there any focus groups working towards reopening the line?' I venture.

'Yes – me,' he laughs desperately.

When I leave him, I take the footpath up through the fields towards Sheldon. Now run by the Society of Mary and Martha, Sheldon offers retreats to support people in Christian ministry, often at times of crisis. It also offers broader private retreats and educational resources. I had visited once as a child, and the atmosphere of the place had stayed with me over the years, so much so that I had immediately thought of it when planning a trip to this area. A short distance along from the village, it is part of Doddiscombsleigh rather than Christow and I remember my father calling it 'Doddy'. The air in these Sheldon fields at this height is pure, like life downed neat, in straight shots. All around, dark green grows and looms and holds and breathes, a living border. Out of this, the Belvedere gleams white – seen from a new angle now, which also seems like a very old one. I wonder if my grandmother saw it from here. And her grandmother.

'Oh, the Sheldon that used to belong to your grandmother's family,' Mum states, matter-of-factly, when I tell her where I have been. Volts flow through. Tingles along the bone.

'What?' I ask, sharply.

'Yes, I think so; ask your father.'

He tells me that my grandmother's family, the Archers, had owned Sheldon for about a hundred years; that it had been bought by Samuel Archer in 1818 and that my father's grandfather, William, had been the last of the family to live there. The Archers had farmed extensively in the Teign Valley, with concentrations in both Christow and Doddiscombsleigh, though it had sometimes been hard to prove the intricacies of their connections.

'The Christow Archers are one of the oldest branches in the Teign Valley, but at the same time the most difficult to trace,' he says. 'There are hundreds of Archers in the records, but it's not possible in more than a handful of cases to work out their relationship to one another and their place in the family tree.'

I think of these ties, knotted and stretched, and the precariousness of our methods of connection. When the archives run out of documents and people with local knowledge pass away, only the land remains. And as even that recedes, will it seem fanciful that there were ever these interlocked lives working and growing in the soil? What happens to them? Will they be entirely displaced, or will some relics remain, like the rusted carriages of a disused train.

21

Under Wood

Before her.
Before her, him.
Before her, him. Before him, holly, elder, willow.
Before her, him. Before him, holly, elder, willow. Before them,
Before her, him. Before him, holly, elder, willow. Before them, us.
  Before us
Before her, him. Before him, holly, elder, willow. Before them, us.
  Before us, nothing.

shhhhhhhhhhhhhhhhhhhhhhhhhhhhhhhhhhhhhhhhhhhhhhhhhhhhhhhhhhhhhh   BE

    pop.   copper. (crop. of. copper.)   BEECH

shh yellow. willow. elder. shoulder. silver. birth. birch. O PEN MAW haw. thorn.

When my father bought the field from the neighbouring farm in the early 1980s, it was yard upon yard of rippling corn. The millions of English acres 'rescued' from their natural state by the Normans were described by W. G. Hoskins as a 'vast area . . . under wood', along with scrubby heath and stony moorland. After the farmer had harvested the corn, my father was left with an expanse of stubble, from which the grass grew up naturally; not from any new seed, but as a pre-existing resident. And the holly grew itself, and the elder; and, rising up the hill from the stream, the bank of willow trees. But the towering firs, the silver birches and copper beeches were planted.

'He used to come back from lecturing in Exeter and dig the holes and we'd put them in together,' Mum says.

'Were they already quite large when you planted them?' I look up at their extraordinary height.

'Oh no, they were small, we never thought they'd get this tall, but then he kept going abroad and the trees grew taller and taller until we couldn't control them anymore. We just let them grow and every now and then cut one down for logs.'

Then he planted shrubs and flowers, so the top half of the field became garden, and the bottom a willow copse. I remember being consulted when he planted a hazel hedge in between copse and garden, to keep the neighbour's goats out. *I'm thinking of making a hazel archway, what do you think?* I nodded furiously, thinking them the most romantic things. And he had sculpted the trees into an overhanging canopy that you could walk through, transitioning from one side of the field to the other. Though I always remember the archway being there, I suppose it must have come later, when the need for the hedge to serve as a goat barrier had ended.

While Hoskins speaks of men in prehistoric and historic times clearing large tracts of woodland by burning trees, and smaller trees and undergrowth by axe and mattock, my father operated more of a live-and-let-live policy, apart from with the flowers. Though this land had been previously tilled by the neighbouring farm and did not require drastic burning or cutting, it had never, at least in the past couple of centuries, been dug for flower beds. These he would dig meticulously, throwing all his weight in. As recently as three years ago, he had drawn plans for the herbaceous beds: intricate plottings of salvia, sage and meadowsweet; rudbeckia, purple flax and euphorbia.

Many childhood holidays had been spent visiting gardens. Arlington Court, Rosemoor Gardens, Greenway and Killerton. He would note the things he liked and transfer them to the field. We both loved the country gardens where herbs and flowers sprouted seemingly randomly among the vegetables. This, he recreated in the field, and pockets of the garden still function this way, though for the most part the vegetables have disappeared. Amid the strains of life then, I remember these garden visits offering a few deep hours of tranquillity.

I ask my father about the garden. He says that both the one here, and the one in Kenya, he really laboured in. Not just dropping in plants here and there, one by one, as and when you had the time, but more of an intense commitment. This surprises me at first, as we didn't have much of a garden where I'd lived in Kenya. I learn, though, that he means his first house in Kenya, in Kangaru, which came with land. When I ask about the process of turning field into garden, he says he went about it 'the Italian way'. I have no idea what this means and press him further. 'Picturesque. And seasonal; asking yourself what you want flowering in the summer and what in winter.' Though it's December now, there is plenty of colour, a testament to this earlier seasonal thinking. And so it is with a developed sense of knowing that I encounter the acers, dogwood and sprigs of barberry that I pick to brighten his room, understanding now how they came to be there.

Now, under this wood, alongside flowers live rabbits, badgers, weasels, voles, squirrels and roe deer. Under this wood live bacteria, protozoa, fungal filaments. Under this wood live clastic sedimentary rocks, evaporite deposits, gypsum. These lay a rocky ribcage under the land. Higher uphill, a flush of sandstone. But here, in the sweep of claystone and mudstone, the soil runs its fine sediment over my fingers. Claystone separates from siltstone through a smooth rub along teeth.

I draw the earth to my tongue, tasting the softness of the rain of hundreds of millions of summers. Just as a wine's terroir depends upon the geology beneath the grapes, the soil can affect the taste of other produce – vegetables, cheese, cider. From my father's small patch of Redlands, I see out the sun with cheese from nearby Quicke's farm, wine from Redyeates, a neighbouring vineyard, and three packets of soil. I have bought the wine from the farm next door that has diversified its farming portfolio over the years, expanding a small shop to a larger one with a deli and café. Successes like this offer optimism amidst fears about changing subsidies, declining workforces, global warming and soil degradation contributing to a new agricultural crisis. Speaking of a time of crisis in the latter half of the nineteenth century, my father had observed how *in the space of a few years the countryside ceased to be a place in which to earn a living, except in the case of a fortunate few.*

The first soil I taste comes from where I am sitting, from the remains of the vegetable garden. It is potent and buttery. The second is from the foothills of the Haldon Hills, at Dunchideock: woody, dense, pine. The last is from Druid's Hill: creamy, grassy, woollen. My father concluded that *whether men realized it or not at the time, it was the end of a way of life that had existed for thousands of years.* Once more the land is changing, along with those who live on and off it. But there is a robustness in the ground that may continue, and pockets – like the acre I sit in – with a future still for tasting, though it may be bittersweet.

22

Vinca Minor ('*Illumination*')

On Christmas Eve, Mum cuts through the muscle of the holly tree that has grown too high, like carving the Sunday roast; she applies herself. I hold the ladder steady; she is slight between the branches. I grip, she saws. Down through the tendons, the tissue. Tree is tough, sinewy, animal. She takes short breaks between sawing.

'I've got it.' She predicts her success. Two small women holding up a tree, cutting it down; and she does it. It falls to the floor, a vanquished body. She never cuts too far, wanting to maintain its foliage for decoration and, perhaps, knowing something of its mythical protective powers. As well as helping to fend off any witches who might happen to be living in the hedgerows, it is often planted close by the house in order to protect against lightning. We now know that the spines of the leaves can actually act as lightning conductors.

We look up together above the absent holly, to the sky which is just turning lemon, and linger in its widely stretching light, only for a moment. Then it is back to the scurrying of jobs, one thing following another, all the way down to the ground where the day hangs heavy in the moss, slumps into cold grass, falling awkwardly on spikes of cones. The day cannot settle: always something nibbling at its ends, work creeping through, clawing us into tomorrow.

I gather up the felled branches, thinking of the battle the Holly King is traditionally thought to have had with the Oak King about who would have dominion over winter. Inside, a battle continues. It is not my fight; I can only lend reinforcements from the sidelines. At the verge, Vinca minor, the periwinkle with variegated leaves, shines amid the day's detritus. I drift into the yellow of its leaves, as it transports the last trickle of day into softly carpeted sea.

In the morning, frost on the fields shines rose-pink. Webs cling to fence posts, to fallen wood: great clouds of silver dust. The sun is high, just over the brow of the hill, spilling apricot. It bounces back off the low grass and periwinkle leaves in a field of Turkish delight. Lemon pours out and glistens the sky which spreads in liquid gold. A flood of sparrows bursts by; a swerve of goldfinches, flash on flash, finch on finch, high in the gold rush.

I break into a run; wetness soars through the toes; underfoot: pine cone, fir, twigs; moss and cinder, blanket of beech, the sigh and sway of oak. I run on a thousand chandeliers, as each blade sparkles with frost; a field of glass underfoot. It is as though the elements are reversed: sky is ground and ground is sky, and I am running on the pinheads of constellations, leaping from star to frosted star. I take deep lungfuls of sun. As I pause to move through some exercises, a robin watches me from its usual hedge. It gives me a look of intense scrutiny, followed by a casual side-eye once it sees that I'm onto it. As I start muttering motivational words to myself, it decides it's had enough and flies away derisively, while I continue, my eyes level with the hills, sun just a little higher. I raise my arms as if in worship, doing sun squats.

I fall back into running, over the ground that my father crossed so many times; do I feel the same to it? Does it recognize the tread? The load? The weight? I feel I could run to the ends of the earth, or the body, whichever comes first. And it is always the body. The heaviness of limbs, the pinch of a pain, breath not coming as fast or as freely; the signs of the body that it cannot keep up with the rhythm of the earth or the speed of the planet. The body calling you back from the sun, from the rhythm of the detached mind, from abandon.

Today I bring him gold. Fringes of oleaster leaves, eleagnus ('limelight'), euonymus ('sunshine') gathered in a gilt-leaved glow.

This is the smoothness of luxury, of not having to work so hard; let it snow through the room in gladdened air, in drifting ease. The glitter of it settling on the furniture; a golden snow that warms as it falls and melts as it stores all the day's light, all the days of days of light.

TWO

23

Warren

One eye first, a half-lid, squint. Both pull fully open. Blue! It had forgotten the breadth of the colour. Sky! The regal spread of it, all-commanding. It pushes up from the soil. First its forehead rises from earth; air laps over it. Nose, lips, chin lift, as if into fresh water. Shoulders, breasts, back. Now it is a rush to get out. Thighs, heels, the back of the neck. Then, a darkness; not black but orange, as the light of its days in the soil stays with it a while, dancing in the retinas. It remembers the warmth, how it cushioned, pulled it down, baked into the folds of the earth. Still. Red. A-glow.

In through the snowdrops, past new spurts of dock leaf, lily of the valley; it longs to return. But in the centre of the copse it finds itself too exposed and moves further down towards the fir trees. Here, it notes the gaping holes of erupted earth belonging to the badgers. Beside them, in a shallow pit, their faeces squat, territorially. Though this is a place it had thought it might stretch, over soft fallen needles, in rooted contours, it seems it is already occupied. Moving over the badgers' turf, through the tent of twigs that the fallen beech has made, it feels this too could be a place to stretch. Up to canopied twigs and the running water of the stream in front. But piles of dark feathers line the bark to the left – the scene of some earlier conflict. A stump of silver birch further down exposes a base fretwork of fungi, and to the right, another blanket of feathers. Rabbit droppings rest like a clutch of eggs; twice it becomes impaled in overhanging brambles. This is not the place.

Down along the stream, a set of pawprints presses into mud: it has not yet moved off the badgers' earth. Here are the only visual traces of the animal it hears but doesn't see. It had first thought their snuffling from the hedge to be a neighbour's horse, though it had seemed to be coming from the wrong side of the border. The snuffling and snorting had continued, interspersed with growls so unnerving it had turned its torch full into the source of the noise. No sudden leap or confusion. When the torch switched off, the snuffling continued, undiminished. It was only then it had thought of the badgers, their dull eyesight untouched by its thin beam. It had read about their calls: chitters, whickers, growls. The whicker, like the whinny of the horse, is often used in frustration; the low rumbling growl: a warning.

It looks up as a fat raindrop lands in its eye. In need of cover, it moves to a leaning oak, whose stretched torso offers a less soluble surface than soil to lie on. Its body fits comfortably against the oak's body. Reclining, it looks up through ivy to the fork of the higher branches, up to a canopy of latticed twigs. Wings pass over. Steady beeps of birds. All the nearby trees strain in this direction. Roots here would get little rain; instead, it would seep in from the nearby stream which is flowing fast and frothing. It would not want to be anywhere else. Everywhere roundabout seems exposed, except for this small bank of trees.

At its feet is a thicket where sloe and holly have nested. It seems the driest place to stretch. As it pulls itself down, ready to navigate into it, it sees a hole in the roots of the tree it has been leaning on. Too large for a mouse, perhaps it's a stoat or weasel. The thought unsettles it. The field is full of them, it knows, from their sound, just after dark. Not witching hour but weasel hour, when the night quivers with their spectral cries. 'Never leave the baby unattended,' its grandmother had told its mother when they first moved here. 'The weasels will have it.' As it gazes into the doorway, it is difficult to know who would be more scared if the owner's head popped out now. As it is, it can only see a couple of inches in, to a crumpled bed of leaves. What looks like a seed rests by the entrance, like shopping delivered to the door. It picks it up, finds it covered in a soft, white, downy fur, then replaces it. It is difficult to find anywhere that is not already taken; where some other animal does not have a prior claim: faeces marking territory; pawprints; the open holed doors of non-human homes.

It gathers itself up and moves back up the field in search of a less claimed resting spot. Rain builds. It is entirely reliant on trees for shelter. Some are not so welcoming: the willows rise tall and lean, with no warmth to spare; others take it to them, fully maternal. The fir beckons with outstretched leaves and presses towards it. When it loosens itself slightly from its hold, it notices it is near a large oak it has known since childhood. A whole family is sheltering here. The blackbirds in the oak's lower reaches; halfling human by the trunk; little flittings in the thicket. When the rain lightens enough to move past the tree's protection, it nudges some branches by its base. Hair tangles with twigs and rain spots its skin like a deep cleanse.

Inches from it, the long-tailed tits bounce and peer but don't retreat. The nearest one, about two inches away, inclines a muzzy head of white feathers, glints black eyes. Then, out of nowhere, sings. Little electronic bird beats, like the start of a trance track. It is surrounded by these beats, like little crickets chirping, a tinny warble. It realizes these are the birds it always hears in the Ide hedgerows. Though it can't bear to leave the sound, the rain has thickened and the wind is whipping into it. It starts to move and the tits flutter back further in the thicket. By the time its body is out of the twigs, their singing has stopped and it glimpses them fluttering further out to field.

At its feet, spots of crimson mushrooms gleam. With their waxy texture, completely out of place in their surroundings, they seem to ask if it couldn't try harder to be a fixed point, to root. Their brazen scarlet caps embolden, and it thinks that perhaps, after all, this is what it could do: find a piece of land to lie in; to make its own and to claim. Not to fight the badger or the bird or the weasel, but to lie alongside them, to coexist. It finds a patch, underneath a thatch of sloe, a burst of white, wet flowers; lies over a covering of ivy and looks up. But there is barbed wire here from some earlier enclosure. Grown over, gnarls rusted to the colour of brambles, the wire catches at its hair. It has to slide itself out and then around, in through a different entrance. To manage this, it must exit rear-first. Growing closer to soil is teaching it so much about movement; it is using so much more of the potential of its body.

The next entrance is smoother. It trails out its fingers and seeps and spreads into sloe, to the white trailing blossom, to bramble. The fingers, the arms, the legs; spreading into earth, into soil, into wetness. It is entering its dreams. Its dream body. Snowdrops. Not thin or muscled or beach-ready, its dream body is stretched and wet and snowdropped. From the tip of an eye it sees a bird's nest. It feels dizzy, though it is lying flat on the earth. It is not used to so much 'up'. It lifts an arm to the nearest branch and holds on to steady itself. A nettle nudges its nose, its hands brush over ferns, its fingers want to touch everything. The caress of moss over branch, the slenderness of twig; it feels more careful of everything it touches, now that it is touching it.

Fingers press down into earth, deeper and harder they probe. It is a burrowing animal. Indents for its heels, for its elbows. Strips of woven soil it slips on like gloves. Head nestles back, through dock and leaf, back; through red open pores, back. Until its ears are in the earth and it is conscious of how many animals have better hearing. And it flaps and tilts until its ears are against the earth and what can they hear? What can they pick up? Who has a heart in the soil? Who, a pulse? Who has the ripple of muscle or burrowing root? Grass tickles. Producing ultrasonic sound waves with higher frequencies but shorter wavelengths, the distance between one wave and the next is smaller than with normal sound. If grass has a voice, it is fast and scorns punctuation. whoisitwhatisitsbodyitsecho-ingspaceisithollowisitrungisitgrassorwomanisitoneo-fussprungfrommusorwhoisitwhatisit Its ear speed-reads the field's voice.

And so it comes to live in the carved-out red, in the tangled root hairs, in the scooped-outness. It lives in the opened space. Where a storm uprooted beech and oak, earth blazes. It is a strange sort of inside-outness.

It finds it has lost its cuticles, as water pours through thin starch-storing veins. At its heart, a star: the xylem; and the phloem lies between the points of the star. It lies back in the bank, in the crumbled earth, in the dense gathering of organisms, of processes. Living in the soil is thick and raw, and the Grassling claws in the hair of words. The grass's speech, the birds' high beep, rabbits' low feet, churning. Imagine a thickness and a brightness together: hold them there. Add the slowest twisting root. Add the writhe of the worm and the coiling of hair and root and worm, and through all of this the pink licks like an animal.

24

Waymark

It is the time of the black hill. Dark on dark, in the part of the morning that is still night, Haldon Forest is obscured. To my left, Exeter's artificial lights shimmer like a funfair. But it is the dark that draws. Birds breeze a song along the top line of the night. Invisible lines shift air into music: a bass of blackness; light treble of bird. Hill starts to separate from sky. I look at the woods that have always been the mark of my periphery: the edge of all my movement. As a child, I would see them as I approached my grandparents' home. Too far to get to, they had seemed an impossible stretch of wildness. Later, as an adult, there were brief visits. Once, I had taken an exhibition of ecopoetry inside, in the converted forest-office building that stood for a time as a gallery. But these were only pricks on the lid of the forest. Now I go on its own time, into its darkness.

The dead are here. Ghosts. Not just the trees, who exceed our human lifespan. Not just the ground, that exceeds even the trees. Not just the rock or the molten insides. But those spirits that take over the body. I walk with the dead. Always, but more so here. Here they are stronger, or my resistance is weaker, or the separation that guards the self is dissolving as I am walking. I feel that the ways people unravel are tiny. And seem tinier in cities. In rooms. In speech, with the words of only one species. Let's unravel in big ways. In big dark. In big tree. In big, dark, bark. Let's lay our ribs out one by one on big ground. *Let me do it for you* (I whisper through the trees, across the fields to him), *since you cannot get out. And I don't want you to, yet, because if you do, your dissolve might not be big but total and I want to keep some of you here. So let me unravel this way, partway, for you. Let me breathe all this gathered life in, and pass it on.*

Climbing the hill, closer to the bank of mist swirling around the deep blue forest, it is easy to think of stepping into another realm. When the Belvedere's white ears poke up, it is closer than I think possible, having always seen it from a distance; an untouchable monument. The view from this height is stunning. Rolling fields, nips and tucks of houses, and along the horizon, the long light of the Exe. Clusters of blackthorn glow like snow trees, shaking their soft flaking flowers. As I near the Belvedere, spits of quartz shine up from the ground, reminders of the land's mining history.

As I come out in front of the tower, I marvel at how a building with so much grandeur from a distance can be so small up close. I look through the windows. It is a daring trespass, like looking in on a different century; or at myself, thirty years younger, awestruck, from the valley below, egging myself on. A chandelier dominates the main window and curtains are tied back in the upper one. As I scan, left to right, up and down, backwards, forwards, I can only conclude that emptiness is its overriding feature. Where now is the love that built it? That drew Sir Robert Palk to commemorate his friend, Major General Stringer Lawrence, through this monument? Has it slipped through the walls, out into the shift of cloud passing fast behind it, or is that what sweetens the air, that overpowers, like nothing else I have ever been soaked in? Walking around the tower, I spot a song thrush singing all-out from high branches, beak lifted vertical into sky. Tilting my head to follow it, it seems entirely possible that love could rise from any structure – a heart, a throat, a tower; could send its vibration into the air, changing its particles, which mutate into a beating sky that lightens all who move through it, that can never more be contained.

Moving further down along the road, I come finally to a trail, and move into its rhythm: Scots pine after Scots pine; woodpecker over woodpecker; the same noise, the same tree, the same steps.

When I cross a line of pylons, I sense strong static: a throbbing density like a noise too high to hear pulses through. I find it hard to breathe. As I walk through the disused quarry, I don't know if I'm meant to be here. I feel electro-magnetic, as though I would stick to anything I touched. Dead tree stumps litter the ground like a graveyard, the antithesis of the dense green pines I was in only minutes before, and I want, desperately, to be out of there.

Then, a sense of another presence. Though it can't last much more than a second, a thousand things seem to happen at once. Slight danger; danger recedes; friendship; a reaching out; eyes: two, four, six, twenty; fur; fear; reassurance; doubt; reaching out; fear; flight. The deer run. I follow. There are rivulets along the forest floor; pine cones and deer droppings, freshly fallen. I need to keep low to move, as the branches of the pines start lower here, growing wilder, untended. I bend and move forwards, almost doubled over. Every now and then, a pool of gleaming water. I follow, until distracted by a tinkling off-trail. The deer move fast ahead, where I see them cross over the path. They are black. Darker than I have ever seen them before. They blend into the violets in the banks where I let them continue on alone, deeper in.

If I were an ancient Briton, I would choose here to settle. Along the flitting stream, in the forest that has always marked the edge of my knowing, a dark waymark of the limits of my movement. Passing through moss and water, pine and bird, I could be at the ends of the earth – and I am. The ends of my own earth. But if I have reached here, what then? Like Jim Carrey in his boat in *The Truman Show*, I have reached the edge of the water. Or the barrier in *The Hunger Games*. I have moved past them. But what then? Then, you forget borders. Not just reimagine them, but truly forget that there ever were such things. And there is no reason you should not go anywhere.

I move up, past the stream, higher than I have ever travelled. Past the glinting water through the trees, the estuary, the sea beyond. Everything limitless. Here, I practise being pine. Arms stretched above my head, breath moving up through the body. Tall and thin and wise, straight down the line, truthful, trusted, solemn and knowing. I wave down to myself, where I have been before and will be again. Now, tree-esque, I tell myself to be poised and that wisdom is just a state of mind, or tree. I am filled with the confidence of coils of age and stature. I don't know why I ever doubt myself or why I wouldn't always choose to stand tall when I have my pick of postures.

This freedom is a feeling I recognize for its rare value; that I will try to carry with me wherever I go, out of this forest. In the times that lie ahead, as territories narrow and common borders close, I will think of this forest. The clumps of moss, the cool water, the hills that hold. To remember this: being up, where I always dreamed of being, whenever I land against something telling me I shouldn't be there.

25

Whisper

whatisitdoingshouldwecatchitshouldweholditwhatdoesitthinkitis-
doingshhhhwehearitspeakitsstoloncreepsitsculmimprintswithsound-
risingfromandintobreakingground

February is the time of the firsts. First snowdrop. First
lamb. First sloe. Slips of white in muted days. First
feet. A lamb runs to its mother. First knowledge of
legs. First speed. First daffodil. First cluster. First field.
First prolonged day, as a light turns on its yellow. First
cherry. A dust of pink in the branches. First blush.
First crocus. First deep colour. The lamb falls. Rises.
First cry. First sound from the body. This is what it
sounds like in air. This is what it is like outside its
body. First baa. First bee. First bud. In the camellia.
First flower. First sweetness in the soil, lifted, its
clumps soaked in open narcissus swimming over the
opening soil, the scent, the deep springing lungfuls.
And though cold and though rain and though cold
and though rain – a white and a yellow. And through
cold and through rain, through cold and through rain
– a pink and a purple. A chaffinch sneezes. Colour
approaching like a storm.

Buzzards come. One swoops overhead. Two.
Weightless. They cry and pass. Five. Circling, swirling together feathered. Up. One's wings fold in like
a concertina as it plummets down, pumping the air

to its advantage. There must be more ways to move the body through air, more ways to play it. It flaps its arms. Grounded, it doesn't make much difference. But what if suspended? Bungee-jumping while pumping the arms might give some approximation, up to the point of the ping back up. It looks round for a smaller experiment. Flapping the arms and jumping on the spot is just a poor woman's star jump. Then, as it moves, the ground swells with wind. Air knocks against the back of its legs, whips against its hands and through its fingers. It climbs onto a bench. It jumps and flaps. Conscious of its weak back, it worries and swells. For a moment, it feels fat in the air, fattened by air, p(l)umped. Landing is strained. Its spine ticks.

Its next target is a tree stump. Too high to climb onto conventionally, first it sits on it, then moves its legs up, one after the other, folded under. In a contorted squat, it ripples up through the body, until standing. The narrowness of its dais is alarming, and even its hip-level height – to one with vertigo – feels uneasy. It takes all its nerve to flap as the wood rocks. It leaps and lands in the knees, forgetting to soften the legs. None of this the buzzard has to worry about, who lands on pillows of air, who drops and floats without a jolt.

Finally, it reaches the fallen beech, which has been its goal since beginning this buzzarding. Fairly easy to climb and backing onto a river, the beech draws it to its possibilities. But it is impossible to climb in wellies. It takes off boots, then socks. Bare-footed, it lifts itself onto the gnarled wood and wet, trailing ivy. It is stabbingly cold. Lifting up through the body it glances down into the water. Balking, it decides on a dummy run on warmer ground first. It swivels round and starts to flap. Falling this time is softer, into beech leaf, speckled ivy, loosened bark. But the flapping motion is not bringing it the buffeting of the buzzard. It starts experimenting with other movements and discovers that moving the arms forwards and back instead of out and in gives much more dramatic results. As the arms swing, momentum gathers; it could fall off the planet. A sheep watches it through a gap in the trees, bemused. Back onto the beech, it faces the river. Arms start forwards and back, inveterate slalom air-skier. But it feels too fast and risky. It switches back to flapping. It falls. Through water. Through mud. Through mud. Deeper than deeply it falls. It forgets to flap. Arms automatically streamline, ready to brace. It lands, eye-level with the sheep. Its body shoots along the ground. There is softness everywhere. In the legs, in the eyes, in the wool, in the water. In the suctioning squelch of the earth. The sheep pulls a little further in front of its lamb. Protective, against this questionable human behaviour.

As it makes its way back up the hill, the wind reaches full pitch. It is pushed back down the brow of the hill; as it lifts, arms begin to pump again. It fills with air. Whole body: hollow. Air in the bones. Light channels up and down its body, pausing at the joints; flooding into the space of the knees, ankles, elbows, collarbone. The joints are places of safety, where light pools and a sea pulls and lulls, translucent. Nothing bad will happen here, in the nodes, along the stem. The body is readying, carving out space and flooding it. It is full of cradles. It fills with fir and moss and drops. The softness of caressing wings, of eucalyptus and snowdrops swirling into veins, of the skull filling with daffodils. Hair shimmers and strokes the air where it lands. In these moments, the body is a different thing, and so is the earth. Not so bound into borders, they drift among each other: body and earth; air and body; body and bird. Internal, external; feeling, imagining; sound, stillness. It is impossible to give up when you know it can be like this: less bordered, more scented, less bound, more connected.

And language, too, is a shifting spirit. All the potential of air in the mouth, the knees, the elbows. An orchestra of bones shuffle, waiting to be touched. The Grassling's stem, low against ground, rustles where it brushes earth, trailing its pressed-in sound. Rune. The Germanic root of the word lifts. '*Run-*': a whisper. A way of speaking into rock or wood is rising from the past. The body, a whispered language, falling gently into grass.

26

Wills

She   *Open*

Sheep   *softly open*

Sheep-steep   *it blushes softly open*

Sheep-steep, steeped   *soil as it blushes softly open*

Sheep-steep, steeped in   *the quarried soil as it blushes softly open*

Sheep-steep, steeped inside the quarried soil as it blushes softly open.

It is quite casually that my father reveals, 'Of course, John Wills was your relation, you know. Granfer Wills your grandfather used to call him.'

'He sounds like quite a character,' I observe coolly, like a police officer interviewing a witness and trying to remain impassive so as to not lead them in any particular direction.

'Oh, he was,' he continues. 'He had a great handlebar moustache. There was a photograph of him but your grandmother threw it out.'

A pull had come from my father's *History*, drawing me to this character's walks across the Ide fields. *From Hayne he would walk to Halscombe across country, crossing the Ide brook, the railway line and passing to the side of the quarry at West Town.* Even before I had known of any connection, I had followed his paths and told my father of the places I had passed. It had pleased him to hear of them, since he remembered the routes from his own childhood walks and liked to learn how they'd changed, or what remained. The audacious wayfaring of this walker also appealed. *Often he*

*would take his hook with him and if he found it difficult to cross
over a hedge, would use his hook to make a stile.*

'He must be your, let me see now, would it be . . . great-
great-grandfather?' It is a delicious moment: a surprise symmetry
uncovered, through the imagination, stumbling on fact. When I
had read the name Wills, I hadn't made any connection, as this
was a relation through marriage – the father of the wife of my
great-grandfather – and so bore a different name. I think about
this slipperiness of names. Lately, when close to the ground, I have
sensed an older naming: the runes of a forgotten language, still
somewhere imprinted. I have felt the weight of these buried words
that may only need brushing to be uncovered. And now I know
that I must act, must follow the whole of Granfer Wills' path across
the fields to see what more the ground might yield. *There is still a
footpath, now designated as 'public', which cuts across the corner
of the field,* I read. *Opposite Hayne in the direction of Halscombe.*
Was it John's hook that laid this ground open?

When I reach John's stile, everything stops. Woods, hills, sun spill
into every spot of retina, flushing everything else out. Head takes
slow panoramic turns, again and again – lazily, not wanting it to
end. The word 'breathtaking' originated between 1875 and 1880,
my father's notes on John, around 1891. The word seems to have
grown in this place. In the winter sun, the woods sing out as sweetly
as they ever could, frosted leaves glittering the ground.

It is a story of work that took John across country, to labour in
the neighbouring farms: Halscombe, Black Hat, Mount Entrance
and the estates of Culver and Perridge. It is labour of a different
sort that brings me, taking my tiny sheep-steps down the hill, trying
not to topple over. As I totter forward I'm aware of all the things I
am trying to keep from falling; the tension of this in the body; the
life I am willing to keep. Though my father is teetering on this side
of the ground, he is here. *A moment more*, I whisper to him across
the fields: *and for as many moments as you can.*

A sudden storm comes in while I'm in John's field. The steep track flattens out halfway down and I sit, protected by the top of the hill, waiting for the rain to pass. The field wraps itself around more snugly than clothing and I let my head fall into grass. The scent at this level is deep and ovine; I burrow deeply into it, surrounded by a nest of grass and hair. Despite excellent peripheral vision, sheep can suffer from wool blindness if they haven't been shorn around the face. Thickets of hair, always tightly tangled with African heat, now mingle with woollen grass and a beating wetness. I see only rain.

When it eases, I continue down the hill, crossing the brook and pausing at another stile. As I take a swig of water, I remember John's preference for a different drink. *He was an expert at cider-making. On one occasion he had promised to be home from Halscombe by eight. Eventually his wife came looking for him and found him lying in the orchard hedge fast asleep, overcome by the drink.* The water tastes of milk and manure, a potent cross-contamination caused by proximity of bottle and umbrella in my bag. I think he had the better idea when it came to lubrication.

Walking along the old railway line, metres down in the felled-out earth, my blood rushes at seeing what is ordinarily invisible: the scooped-out insides of the soil. Its gleaming red gushes like a wound I walk through. Its sides jut into rock and fern, ivy clings onto everything; all of them pressing at the earth's weak point. Brambles hang down as rope from a higher canopy, while uprooted tree carcasses lie on their sides, majestic bodies on a battered battlefield.

As I first come upon the rock face of the old railway bridge – strewn over with ivy, gaps of blackness spotting between stones – I feel something like awe. Though it is not fear that holds me fixed, immovable, but the suddenness of history stepping out in front of me. Here is something that men built. That living bone and sinew hauled and handled. A disused space carries its past with it, does not entirely give up its use value after it's discarded. I see the men that built this bridge and railway, as much as I see the stone before it. I feel connected to them through my father, though I don't believe any of my relatives worked on the railway. But those who did may have known my family. What if they brushed past them in the street, in the pub? I wonder how this hollowed space affects others; if it's only me that sees these bygone people.

My father recalls the owner of Exeter House in Ide, at the time of writing the *History*, as being *very conscious of the atmosphere of the place. He has described to us how at times he has imagined that the downstairs rooms, where the bar-parlour must have been, are crowded with people dressed in the costume of a century and a half ago*. My father takes this backward glance even further, suggesting that *perhaps what he can see is one of the Parish or Vestry meetings that were held here frequently and these are the farmers drinking on an Easter Monday when they had just finished dealing with the depressing business of doling out poor relief to the paupers of the village*. It is one of the rare flights of fancy that he allows himself in his research, one of the *what ifs* that float through his work.

They fall in here, the little *what ifs*, settle in the cracks amid the stones, in the sinking subsidence of the soil. And in this soil is fine-grained breccia and sand. And in this breccia are clasts of soft purple-weathered vesicular lava and purple-weathered basalt. And in this lava is the story of the gentle stretching of the earth's crust after the compression of the Variscan orogeny ceased, millions of years before the railway, before John, before any human structure, any human life.

27

Withy

See the shell smashed in some curious knot like an offering. See the colour of sand sprinkled, the mistle thrush's egg laid open. All the empty spaces call to all the empty spaces. Perhaps, after all the hollowing, something will hold. Perhaps, after all the fallowing, something will grow. Or perhaps that is only something that happens to other people. Perhaps now there is only this body: a place that someone used to inhabit which is now just a placeholder, left open for whatever should happen to make it back.

It goes to all the absent spaces: the shells that birds have flown from, the flattened leaves the deer has moved off, the ruptures in the bank from rabbit, stoat and weasel, the indents in the soil along the withy beds. Even the word 'withy' is only a film of what it used to be, an older form for 'willow', passing out of use. From the Old English *wīthig*, to Middle English *withye*, through to 'withy', the word waits, with nothing to do now that willow is here. It lies among the branches, where it knows it once was welcome, where it knows it once had a use.

The withies, without the man who planted them, seem leaner, skeletal; in a sea of wooden icicles. Covered over with frost, the Grassling's limbs rattle and scrape against their wind-blown bark. It wonders if

someone struck a mallet – against it, against them –
what frozen music might chime. But nobody does.
There is no full-bodied contact here, just a restless
shivering. The marks beneath the withies from the
press of passing paws hold it there the longest. It feels
the shadows of hooves, leaves, fingers run all over –
trailing, testing, touching. Some of them try to work
out what it is, rolling it over and over between thumb
and forefinger. Others just want to move past, using
it as the quickest route on to somewhere else. It bristles with each passing.

It imagines itself without him. It has to. What then
will the body be? Not an upright frame, that is certain. A sagging slump. Amorphous. There is no water
in the pond. It is covered over with dry sticks, rotting
vegetation hanging in solid cobwebs. The odd boggy
patch. Skins have broken and bodies poured out.
Slumps of fat and gut. Muscle stretched out of shape
and discarded. Intestines curled like worms, disturbed.
Proteins, fats, simple carbohydrates will be the first to
go, leaving the more fibrous cellulose, lignins, tannins.
Most will disappear in a matter of weeks or months,
but for some, it will take years. New matter will form,
as the micro-organisms excrete organic compounds,
themselves adding to the organic matter after death.
These excretions and decomposing remains form
humic substances in the pond sediment, similar to
humus in soils, slow to decompose. Is that what the
body will be? Slowly slopping under, slapping its skin
against mud, flailing and flapping, waiting for a hook
to land it.

It can either catch itself or let itself be caught. Not
sinking but saving. There is something in the ground
before this picking off of flesh; in a different layer,

another part of the cycle. It glints, now and then, from the pieces of a shell, or the pristine sheen of a withy. It calls the Grassling until its stem brushes against the whispering runes, the pulsing of moons, the grass overheard, the Old English words; it is a densely wooded speech. Even when it can't hear it, it often now senses its light, or feels its movement. It has learned where language lies, with buried trinkets in the ground, intermittently breaking the surface.

It puts out a hand. Words begin to rise. Verbs pelt. Move. Lift. Sound. Swim. Things start to happen. It listens to the motion in the ground. The thump and the leap, the dart and the creep, a rock writhes, a eukaryote dives; all of this is happening. The slow pull of a worm along its crumbled bed. The secretion of its chemical sentences. The actinomycetes, bacteria and fungi, also changing the chemistry of the soil. The ants, beetles, centipedes, millipedes, mites, rotifers, snails, spiders, springtails, slugs; biting, sucking, tearing away at it. All of this is happening. The leaf leaves behind its lignin, its midrib, laid out in the path like a tooth in a glass. The fungi breaks down the rib, the feather-winged beetle eats the fungal spores. The ground beetles crunch at snails and chew at slugs. The clover comes away from itself. Things are leaving and things will not be the same. He is leaving and it will not be the same.

Now they are clamorous. Words honk and cry, in bellows. It wants to take their air out. It wants to draw them out from the ground, haul them out onto the grass and say: Quiet. Here are pieces of a shell that cannot be put back together. Quiet. Here are holes all over that will not close. Quiet. Here is a dead bee, its wings flecked with gold like stained glass windows laid flat in a mossy cathedral. But the ground will not let it. The ground sees that it is only masquerading at emptiness. That it is a living thing that will fill again. Sun, air, scent will come back, even sound. You cannot till the body. What will grow will grow regardless. What will leave cannot be made to stay.

28

Wooded Fort

'Is Granfer Wills buried in Ide Church?'

'No, Dunchideock,' my father reveals. 'A peaceful place. I'd like to go back there sometime.'

As I make my way along the lane, my lungs fill with the scent of my grandparents. Visits to their house in Dunchideock always smelled like this. I look round for the source and see high yew trees behind a laurel hedge and remember how the laurels had required constant trimming, a particular and ongoing concern of my grandmother's. As the smell disperses, so does the memory and I refocus on what is around me. Past the laurels comes the church. It is Grade 1 listed and a very smart affair. On this occasion its red tower built from local sandstone blazes against the evening light. As always when entering a graveyard, tasked with finding a particular stone, I am jittery. How will I find it among so many others? How will I manage not to step on someone? And always the undertone of trespass. 'Ever so sorry,' I hear myself saying as I land on someone's shoulder.

The only Wills I see is on the other side of the church, but the stone bears the wrong first name and date to be John's. During my survey, I keep an eye out for some of the more interesting burials noted by local historian Archie Winckworth. His list provides an eclectic mix of accomplishment and folly, including a 'Direct descendant of Sir Walter Raleigh', someone who 'In his Will left "My beloved wife the bedstead"', another who 'Corrected the works of Sir Isaac Newton' and one who 'Attended Church as a child with a placard on [its] back [reading] "Pray for me. I am a liar"'.

I may well have missed John in my rapid search, racing the light, not wanting to still be out walking the lanes in the dark. As I look up to a line of crows, something swoops across the lane. Speed. Darkness. It is unfolding. Width. Hands in its wings. Fingers in its sides. Touch made multiple, drawn out wide. Silent. Higher than the trees, or the stretch of an eye. It passes over like a chill, a trillion raised hairs, a glitch in the matrix. Did I see something I shouldn't have? A different kind of life, where touch is prioritized, where fingertips stretch down the ribs and stick to other bodies like Velcro?

A greater horseshoe bat's wing bones are mostly hand-bones and most of its body is its wings. Its speech is often too high for humans to hear. A whole species covering the earth through touch and sound, with no interest in speaking to us. But the greater horseshoe needs cattle-grazed pastures, hedgerows, broad-leaved woodlands, diverse grasslands; in short, a helpful human stewardship of the soil. At West Town Farm, a few miles down from here, there are bat boxes, encouraging safe spaces to roost, and marked trails for walkers to look up and view them. But bats come out at dusk, after many walkers have safely returned home; and they seem altogether different to the kind of animal you might stand and stare at. The only mammal to fly, really fly, can do so many things better than we can. They move faster than we can see and speak higher than we can hear. You do not watch or hear, but feel them.

I know what it is to travel at speed. Back into my father's memories, into Granfer Wills' footsteps, into traces of places. Sometimes it is a material movement. And to have part of my body raised to the light but part anchored below ground is a difficult balancing act. Sun floods lightly from the top down, wisps around my fingers, feathers my pores. It is like trailing a hand in the sea, in the wide, unending blue, pressing fingers down into water. Sunlight strobes, as though over seaweed, as skin dips, in and up; while an opposing current runs down along the leg, the toe, the root, down against rock. Other times, it is just the mind that moves. That swings back and forth against the head, barely coming to rest.

As I cover the last bit of road, the fields throb with owls. Their willowy warble shakes the air, one after another, after another. I hope they are not passing on the whereabouts of the bat. For tonight at least, I hope it swoops safe over the woods to roost, telling stories of its travels in its private language that we cannot speak.

When I wake to the hills my father woke to year after year of his life, I am acutely aware of the top of my body. From my head, down my neck, to my shoulders, there are invisible strings, tethering me to the floor. My ribs rock with birdsong. It is a peaceful place, he had said, and I feel it. The land accepts me without question; sky too, as it bustles its pink in over the horizon. Day! Day! It surges and spills, flooding me with blushing lightness.

Then comes the sun. A golden wash over everything. Like the flashback or plot twist that makes you realize you are only just now seeing things the right way, this colour makes a mockery of all the light that has come before it. This is the daylight. This is how things are meant to be seen. The trees that extend their golden veined fingers to me are older than Granfer Wills; he would have seen them too. Just then, the clip of horseshoes clatters in along the path and little separates this scene from one he may have seen.

I follow the horses along to the church where they part ways. If John is here, today I will find him. I enter the church and am relieved to find a map of the churchyard layout, 'based on plan of March 1958'. I scour the names attached to each plot, but the only Wills I see is the one I had found before. However, it seems a very large plot, compared to those around it: the length of about four regular ones. I wonder if John could have snuck in somewhere there.

Returning to the gravestone, I see Joseph's name and Elizabeth's underneath. Pushing back the ivy, I uncover another one: Emily, and just make out the word 'Daughter'. Further down, at the very bottom of the stone, the ivy gives up one final name, something like 'Walter'. Still no John. Even if he's not here, there is clearly a clan of Willses, who I spend a moment talking silently to. As the mist rolls off the Haldon Hills in waves and the sun starts to break through, it seems like a pretty good spot to come to rest.

As I walk back towards Ide, my father's prediction returns: *it seems possible that . . . pockets of Romano-British settlements survived in the Haldon Hills.* I look behind to where the rain is held over the black trees. He grows in confidence as he expands: from 'possible' it becomes 'likely' that *the south-western edge of the later parish of Ide, lying immediately below the Haldon Hills, provided a home for a small British settlement long after the conquest of the rest of Devon by the Anglo-Saxons.* I warm to this defiant longevity. Though there are few place names in Devon that pre-date the Anglo-Saxons, Dunchideock, meaning 'the wooded fort', is one of them. I hold my father tight inside this place, this fort, the gathered sap of over a thousand years, as the mist heaves in white, like rolling snow.

Little flicks of white kick in and out of the hedgerow, as long-tailed tits rattle and trill. To the right, a flash of ruddy feathers hovers and floats. It lifts and falls along the air streams, weightless. It must be a hawk, but is not one I am familiar with. As I move closer, it glides upwards on an air current, as effortless as a kite. Kite. Red. Red kite. Once extinct in most of the UK, the red kite was reintroduced as part of a release programme in 1989. It's now an amber conservation priority, rather than red, showing its progress; though it's not thought to be particularly established in Devon. The birds introduced as part of the release scheme have been tagged; I can't see a tag on this one. Could it be part of a native population? It is a landscape of survival, of beating the odds. After one more blast of breast, the colour of the soil beneath it, it glides further into the field, away.

Then, a flurry of movement across the fields. It's a bounding, animal motion and for a moment I think they are horses, that a race or hunt is mid-flow. But as I focus, I see they are smaller and that no people are involved; four deer lope across the lime grass into the copse at the end of the valley. I want to watch after their little white bobtails, but traffic is busy here and cars unsympathetic to me standing in the road. I want to go on watching and to go on being a part of this scene; this glimpsed wildness now hidden in the trees that nobody else knows is there.

The rain that has been threatening finally catches up with me at Markham Cross, the place now known to me as the land of the harriers. Here I shelter against the hedge until the sun starts to break through. I shift my feet back and forth, lightly over the earth. If I were fungi, I could absorb this light and pass it onto those around it. I feel myself soaking in sun, but cannot yet pass it on. I stretch my fingers, tangled in ivy, moss and twists of bark. I want to help the things I touch but am not yet close enough, am still too separate. Yet, as I watch a lamb gambol as only a lamb can, not worrying that it is not earth or grass, it suddenly feels quite wonderful to have a body. A moving thing that can show itself visibly, that can state publicly that this is what it is. That can gather all of itself up at once and gambol on at a moment's notice. For a moment, I am satisfied being separate.

Then I think of my father. From this vantage point he advises: *look back over your shoulder across the land belonging to Pynes farm to modern Ide and then down over towards the estuary and the Cathedral in the distance . . . Here are the origins of a settlement which disappeared (or almost disappeared) some two thousand years ago.* I think of him as he lay, the only movement his breath: in, out; taking in the air that came through the open window from his acre, from the far fields, from – here? Is this where he came when he couldn't be found? Like the red kite, or the unearthed rocks of ancient homes, did he find himself tethered to this place? *Almost disappeared.* But, as all hardy perennials lost in the autumn, he had returned.

29

Words

To be blown away. To have nothing to shoot down, nothing coming from the body but air. Nothing tethered, nothing stable; all outward facing, outward casing; chasing only an outline of a body. It is like this for weeks. Moving only through corridors, sticking to the corners of rooms, edging out only when it has something heavy to weight it down. It starts filling its pockets with stones. It stops wearing clothes. In place of skin there is a rough covering people start to see through. It is a colour that doesn't know a name.

It becomes cautious in fields. It could be easily stepped on, or eaten. There is little to differentiate it now from the other stems, except that it is less stable. It notices that others do most of their moving below ground, while it still does most on top. Perhaps that is the trick to not being so precarious in air: to do more of its work underground. They group together; it seems to be the only one out alone. It wonders what they're doing huddled up like that. Are they talking or are they listening or are they dancing or are they thinking? Or is it some new activity that lies somewhere in between?

It watches their bodies. Some coarse, some smooth, all pumping sunlight in plain view. It thinks of its veins. Is it right to have them inside? Should it reach into its wrist and pull, until the long line of itself unravels, then thread it back together on the outside?

There is so much to learn and unlearn. It likes to see what the others are doing. As it comes to know them, it forgets its fears. It is cautious only outside fields.

Is it a joined-up thing or separate? That, it still can't work out. When it's left to drift across the grass, out and over, out and over, in the cold freshness of the morning, it feels that it could keep going; out and over, out and over, never coming to rest. But then it is checked. A tug at the nape of the neck. A curling finger around a rib. It is brought back. There is something that says it belongs to it. Perhaps it is words. Perhaps it is they that say: I have seen you, I have touched you, I belong to you. Perhaps it doesn't matter which ones are used, perhaps they all mean: I have seen you, I have touched you, I belong to you.

When it is a long way out, their gust up through the ribs and out of the head remind it that part of it is still manageable. That part of it is still very small. That all the space inside it can come, for a second, to rest in the firm shape of a word. There is a comfort in the way they all start and end. The way they have the same things, always, inside them. It can rely on a word to take a strange, shapeless sea and start and end it so glibly, as if to almost make a joke of it: this wide, unstable movement. It takes hold of it and says, *when I place you here and line you up in these pebbles of breath, you become so much less.*

But they cannot be relied on. Sometimes it sees them lined up on the shore while it wings its way over waves, deep and swelling. Their bodies seem altogether too perfect, as it steers its shifting shape against the spray; sometimes flat and flapping as a sunfish, other times with the clipped beat of a bird. Words are too far off, then, to help. Perhaps, at those times, it is a colour that brings it back. The grey sheet of sea over rock, the sky falling into it. The metal. Iron wool rolled flat from moon to water. And in the colour, the cries. The gulls. The long stretch of a sound that says: *I have seen you.* This white sound is in the grey waves and the sound foams and the waves say: *I have touched you.* Sometimes that is what it takes to bring it back.

Or, it is a clutch of daffodils. The sun's petals fixed like the beam of a lighthouse. It is the flowers and the leaves it gathers, shade upon shade, light upon light. From daffodil to euphorbia to forget-me-not: yellow, green and blue. From sweet pea to heather to Michaelmas daisy: indigo and violet. Rover rose. Mountain ash. Perhaps it is the light of a rainbow. These are the things that bring it back when words fail; when they are too far off to harness.

Yet they are there all the same. Lined up at the shore, or buried deep in the soil. They are there, waiting for someone to catch them, and roll them round in a palm of pearls. Some of them – the ones that keep their husks on, the traces of where they have come from – can bring all sorts of things together. Old words spill into new; forgotten landscapes fizz with dew as the word for Druid comes alive in 'drew'.

For the Grassling, words are the nodes of their bodies; the joins that graft. So, however far they may stretch outside them, they have a way, still, of returning. At least for the moment, they have a dirt-speckled alphabet, lifted out of the earth like a row of beans. Whenever either of them goes out too far, one puts out a hand to pull the other back. Their hands dig for letters thrown in piles of what the soil yields. Their days are me su d not by su s but fields nd fi ds an fie ds.

30

Wynn

I take the old route to Ide, with Exeter and the Exe on the left. A train chugs past, drawing its eye to the new university accommodation that is 'new' only compared to my last visits along this road, in childhood. Then, I would be on my way to see my grandparents. I suppose, in a way, I still am. I arrive early at the farm, where the workers are gathered, waiting for the day. Manure and wild garlic mingle as they invite me to take a seat out of the rain. It feels strange to leave my father to come here. To be connecting with him through being here, instead of back there, physically with him. But you still have to go places, do things. Don't you? If you yourself are a moving thing?

An old man waits nearby while I make notes. I could be speaking to him, I chastise myself. Perhaps he has connections to this place. But writing does take you away from things, in order to come back. The man wanders off into a field past some caravans, as I sit, writing, opposite an orchard of young trees, tightly enclosed in triangular boxes.

'She's here now,' he calls over the field, from his vantage point above the car park. 'Thank you,' I gather my notes and follow his gaze to the woman approaching, who looks at me questioningly.

'I'm here for the pottery,' I explain.

'Ah!' she smiles. 'This way.'

We spend the first part of the day warming the barn up and swapping our stories over tea. Somehow, the question of what I want to make today takes me from soil to my father to health to words.

And somehow her answer is her mother and clay and health and hands. I love talking to artists. It's a form of speed-talking: straight to the marrow, without any fat.

'Can I dig some clay?' As I ask, it suddenly becomes terrifically important.

'Yes, I'll just borrow some boots,' she replies with the willing practicality of someone who is used to making things. We stride out into the rain, which is sheeting in off the hill. 'I quite like this weather,' she says, optimistically. She points out various landmarks of the farm as we make their way over to what counts as a quarry. Bits and pieces of the place I already know from walking, and I tell her about Granfer Wills and his footpath. She laughs and says I must speak to one of the others from Organic Arts, a charity that runs farm-based learning and arts projects from the farm, who has collected stories from local people. 'You two should have a conversation!'

They cross over the brook and she tells me that sometimes they lay the willow there, to prepare it for working. I think about that process. Not too dissimilar to my swimming. Lying in any river I can get, hair winnowing out, fingers spreading, readying to become something more than I usually am; to become more of my potential. The quarry is in a circle of land called the Henge, banked by thirteen trees: a Celtic ritual, the man from the earlier field tells us, when he sees us heading off in that direction. 'This is Andy, the gardener.' Lucy had introduced us, so we had got to speak after all. 'They planted them as part of their project,' he gestures over to the group disembarking from a small coach and explains they were from a local mental health charity and came regularly to the farm, to garden.

The Henge is currently overrun, as Andy had warned us, since no one has been there in a while. Lucy points to all the brambles. 'This is what they've come to clear,' she explains. But I'm still ringing with the bells of the Celtic ritual and its symmetry with my own pilgrimages to the neighbouring Druid's Hill. I look at the trees and caress their labels, wishing there was more time to engage with them. 'Elder,' says one, 'Hawthorn,' another. I wonder how they choose the trees.

Lucy dives down into the ditch, straddles the water and pitches with her spade. It is physical work. She shows me the part that is clay. Under grass: topsoil; under this: roots, stones. Here, and lower down, the clay, yellow from shale. I stumble down to her, steadying and scratching myself with brambles. We swap tools: her spade for my bucket. I strike soil. Ground resists. Through the tangled roots and rock, I thump, thump, until a little leeway. I press down on the spade with my foot, leaning my weight into it, still straddling the stream. My foot greets the ground below as something familiar; I have been down this low before. Then, as I strike down, the clay cuts loose: big clumps come away onto metal. I lug it up to Lucy who is ready with the bucket.

She tells me which parts we can use and which parts to throw back. 'We don't want too much rock or too big roots – try there,' she says, pointing at the water. I start digging in water, remembering the balancing act from when I last tried to move down as well as up, bridging the elements. I fear the clay will be too heavy to lift out, with my back weakened from cold-water swimming, but in the end the exertion is no different to being on land. 'Ah, this is the good stuff,' Lucy beams, shaking it loose from water and landing it in the bucket. When we have our fill, we scramble back up the bank, out of the ditch, and over to the barn that is Lucy's pottery.

'We need to work it a little, take out the stones – do you want gloves?' I refuse, wanting the feel of it on my fingers. 'OK, be careful, some are sharp.' I start taking the soil apart. Twines of root, sprinkles of grass, rock: these are all discarded. Once the larger items have been removed it becomes a trickier process; bits of gritty roughness spike the skin. 'Small bits of stone are OK,' Lucy reassures me, as my fingers sift and prick.

'Of course it used to be desert,' she muses, 'thousands . . . I don't know how long ago.' And I am with her, across those aeons of time that can't be measured, not really, in human terms. We just know them as further back than we can ever truly go. She talks about the different geological areas identified on the farm: clay at the bottom of Easterbrook's, the slopes of Ashton Shales, red sands in the Crackington formation along the road, dark red iron-rich materials in the basalt in the quarry, breccia rock along the railway cutting. It is the sandstone in the Crackington formation, the original bedrock of Devon, that speaks of Lucy's desert: vast sands that flowed into Devon's Culm basin after being dislodged by earthquakes. In this Carboniferous period, the first amniotes (vertebrates who laid their eggs on land) came into being. These reptiles were the precursors of both modern birds and mammals. The Burnetts, perhaps, 300 million years ago, were reptiles, adapting to a new life solely on land.

All the while our fingers work, automatic now, removing all obstacles. As the clay starts to come together – no longer isolated clumps of turf and stone but smoother rolls of something continuous – I notice the colour change too. Lighter and lighter it turns, speckled like a starling. And the specks seem like flecks of gold, as if my kneading is a kind of alchemy. 'It's almost gold,' I whisper. Lucy nods and smiles. In the silence, our fingers rise and fall, teasing the gold from the ground. It glistens unbearably, as maddening as beautiful things are: separate, ephemeral, entirely out of our control.

We commune for what must be about half an hour in our golden silence. The clay becomes softer and softer, like a person letting down their guard after constant kneading. 'Do you want to go back out and get some sand to sprinkle in?' Lucy asks, matter-of-factly, like she's used to mining a field any time she wants some seasoning. 'We can get some plants at the same time, to press into the clay.' We pass through the farm's new orchard, over to the old railway line. We talk about the badgers whose openings are every-where, whilst scanning for leaves with good veins that will leave an imprint in the clay. I find a fern and, underfoot, an oak and a beech leaf. Lucy collects odd-looking lichen. Before leaving, we look down the tunnel of the abandoned railway. It's eerie, and truly like a portal. Children's cries come from the other end, a school party being taken on a walk, and reverberate in the space like ripples of time. 'See, the sand is just on the top here,' says Lucy, jolted into sound by the children's noise. She bends down and scoops the topsoil.

Back in the pottery, we dust the clay with the sand. 'It might stop some warping,' Lucy explains. She talks lots more about the heat and potential hazards, but I'm not really concentrating as the bright grains trickling through golden clay shine in little sparks of fire. First alchemist, then fire-starter. These are elemental forces, firing through my hands.

Then we bash the clay about a bit, getting rid of the air before rolling it out. 'This is the fun part,' says Lucy, as we press in the plants and roll them flat. I love the look of it raw, like this, before firing. Embedded in the clay, the fern lies like a fossil, its leaves spread as ancient bones, preserved plant skeletons. The leaves are face up, so the external veins can sink into the clay, leaving their imprint. We play around with different implements. Lucy shapes patterns, while I write. I use a pointed stick, so that writing becomes an act of pointing. My hands move over a time when writing was more like this, with runes inscribed on rock, wood, metal. As I grip the wood, the word *wynn* is conjured through its sap. An Anglo-Saxon letter, lost in modern English, it came from this runic language. A word that represented the letter w. Word. Wood. Wynn. The letters slip between my fingers.

And as the wood pricks into the clay, sometimes smoothly, other times having to pick its way among the grains, it says: look. This is the soil that you come from. This is the soil of your fathers. The wood says, this is your mark in it: here, and here, and here. This is your writing. The wood says, in between the grit, the different bits of ground and grain, the muzzled spits of fallen rain, the root that twists again, again: write this. The wood says, if you don't, who will? Who else knows this soil, fat with presences? And perhaps, if others wrote their earth, perhaps we could have, as soil scientists do, a whole catalogue of charted presences, profiles, in the ground. And reading could be a many-layered thing, a digging thing: a harvest.

As I cut the edges of the clay to turn it into a tile, I see little bits of root sticking out at the seams. I pull on them like thread.

31

Xylology

doesitremembertherainsallthosewhohavemovedoverit-
doesitknowwhentroubleiscomingthereisonlyoneofitsoper-
hapsitdoesn'thavetocompeteperhapsallthesunisitsownbut-
canitcaptureitaloneandwhatdoesitdowithit

X marks the spot
X marks the spot of its join
X marks the spot of its joints.

shhhhhhhhhhhhhhhhhhhhhhhhhhhhhhhhhhhhhhhhhhhhhhhhhhhhhhh
SPEECH
shhh will. ow. (stretch. sloe.) O   black.   BE   SPEECH
shhhhh~~hhhhhhhhhhh~~hhhh   S. OAK.   haw.   THORN   SEECH   SPEECH

It comes to map the copse, to see who is talking to
who, to eavesdrop. It sees it is in an inner circle of six
trees, but it is hard to count which are inside and
which outside; slightly extending the boundary, the
six become sixteen. Then it forgets which ones it has
counted and which it hasn't, dizzily encircled. This
central point has known many interior battles. The
tree immediately in front curves away to the left,
almost doubled over. Most trees are bent the other
way from past storm-damage, but as it shifts to the
tree in front it sees that too has a low branch jutting
out in the same strange direction.

The two craning trees seem to join together at the tip. The top of the branch has grown up towards the leaning tree and their branches clash. As it moves under the point of their join, it no longer looks like one of conflict, but of support. Like the beginnings of a wicker basket that someone has left unfinished, or a magnified, abandoned nest. The branches lock in a wooden embrace. As it follows the tips of them, it notices a gathering of buds. Looking closer, it sees these belong to a third tree. This one is leaning into the embrace from the opposite direction. It is a silver birch, a different species, yet all seem happy interweaved. It breaks off its study as a buzzard comes so low it wonders if it is on its radar. At this proximity it sounds like it's laughing, the wheezy cackle of an elderly man.

Then it's distracted by the pheasant that lands, letting out a loud report to which others of its kind reply from the neighbouring field. Then it's called by the long-tailed tits, burst after burst, they fly their pied wings over like sudden shivers. It wonders what the birds are to the trees. Do trees hear? Can they sense colour? What do they make of their flashy, darting, winged inhabitants? Its spot in the inner circle is dark and cold, as high branches of ivy and tops of birch and willow form a canopy. It looks out with envy to the open floor in front, out towards the stream. If it wants to listen to the trees, it is best to be in them, it reminds itself, not out in the open fringes. Yet the sun is falling like treacle on the ivy outside, and beyond that pussy willows shine like cut glass. It needs to be in the lit space. A plant, straining for the light; it gives in and moves.

It is immediately rewarded, glimpsing a robin swimming in the falling water. It darts under the flat

stream, dips and shakes, before hopping down into
the waterfall. Its panicked flit as it descends seems
to say, 'this was a bit of a mistake'. It has to stop
itself from crying out laughing at the exuberance of
it all and look away. But in the instant that it does,
the bird moves; and when it turns back, it is gone. It
becomes clear that it must abandon the trees for the
birds. The ones who scurry along the grass, the ones
who dip and dart among the branches; those on the
highest tree tips, those in the hedges. Those whose
cries are so throated they are like animals. Those who
are all a-flutter. Those whose singing is a wheezing
that seems to worm out of the wood. Those with a
light tseeping. Those with a call and response; those
with an alarm. Those asking if someone is in; those
passing the gossip. The darters, the divers, the rock-
ets, the swoopers, the jitterbugs; the ones that go off
like a gun. Those who let themselves be seen and those
who don't. How can you listen to anything else? Back
comes the buzzard: weow, weow. The Grassling is so
close to a wren it sees the speckles all along its wing.

Rain settles in the buds; shining little bud-bulbs
turn the tree into a chandelier. Hawks pass overhead,
sending their shrill signals. 'Weow,' one suggests;
'Weow,' another answers. Moving back to the inner
circle of trees, it passes the badgers at the southern-
most tip of the circle, then the stream, then the clump
of daffodils on the border. At its radius is the sloe
thicket where it had stretched a few months ago, tap-
ping on the roots and hearts of the earth, straining to
hear. Though it has not rained for hours, everything
is wet, but it pulls itself down and in. Who is in? It
wonders, who is there? It trails out its fingers. By now,
it knows things by touch. The spring of wet moss, the

papery ivy, the pliable softness of twig. The scarlet elf cups everywhere, little pockets of fire, turning forest into fairytale. It lies among them, feeling the red rise and the pink soar of the land beneath.

As it stretches, it considers itself from above; what might this slow, still life in the ground mean to a buzzard, or passing drone? What if a scientist took its picture now, and uploaded it. Could they use an algorithm to analyse it, to see how it is changing to meet its environment, or how to maximize its growth? It thinks of older methods of land management, how they were gentler and more tied to natural processes. John's father, farming near Dartmoor, ploughing with horses. Mulch in place of pesticides. Fields left to rest while the soil replenishes itself. But these have increasingly been replaced by the methodology of mining, even as this has become more aggressive, with powerful new technologies. And part of it wants to send this field study of a planted woman, resting in the earth, to an agricultural technology corporation to see what they would make of it. But the bigger part of it flinches at this surveillance, curls tighter, stays hidden.

Now, the only sound through the rain is the lambs: a chorus of woollen bleating. Greenfinches dart above from branch to high branch before skipping off into air. Like mobile patches of grass, they gleam and spark. Wet light finds its way to the daffodils, shining them into the foreground. Their bent heads, glistened by rain, hang limp like muted trumpets. It is staggering how completely we forget the rain when the sun comes. Whilst in it, it is impossible to comprehend anything else. Then, greenfinches gabble in the apple tree as the Grassling basks in bright daffodils bells.

It plucks some for its father, realizing a year has passed since its last gift of yellows.

At the still hour of the stilling day, air freshens, sounds settle. Sky starts to blush; bleats blot the air. It uncurls and begins its evening inventory, checking all along the border. Badger, mushroom, stream, flower. Particular trees. The leaning tree, the knot of willow and birch, the fir trees. The fallen tree. It needs to check it's all still there, like phoning home. Even in the wood, little pockets of trees form, huddle together, preferring each other's company. Few stand completely alone. As the sky starts to slit with light, cuts of lemon in the lilac, the tree's leaves darken and whole trees seem to slip into darkness, to be absorbed, or to absorb it.

The trees at this hour seem to come into themselves, or out, out of their barks. To be speaking. As the birds end their sound, the trees take over, speaking through moving; extending their leaves, swaying, resting, rustling. And, with a last shuffle of lilac and leaf, it is dark. It returns to the inner circle and the trees seem to close in. Do they huddle, really – cuddle? It feels like they would accept it here. Given long enough, wrap willow around it, plait each other's hair. It does not want to return to the domestic. It wants to stay and stay and savour each last thing. 'Stay,' they seem to say. 'Stretch,' they seem to say. 'Shhhh sloe shhhh slow

        sOAK   shhhh

shhh will. ow. (stretch. sloe.) ~~shhhhhhh~~hhhh.'
Throats soak in sap. And what conversations need to be had, except these? It won't hear anything as fascinating as these trees.

Something cuts through. A lick of flame as a fox pads across. Stops and sniffs. Does it smell the Grassling? It admires the regal point of its nose as it takes the air. Lifts its own nose to wind as the fox does. Wonders how its own body smells, swarming with sap and soil. Red ears prick against a backdrop of dark hills. Head pivots: left, right; missing the Grassling, before a full head-turn brings them face to face. They look into each other for five, ten, twenty seconds before the fox darts, disappearing into land's edge. What passed between them? It thinks, a kind of softness.

Then how does one pick oneself back up, out of the earth? Return to the inside of buildings, having been inside the soil? To people who do not pass on nutrients, but bloat and hoard and fence. It is harder to do these things out in the open. Out without fences. Out without borders. It is harder to hoard, lying flat and stretched on blossoming earth. But there are still neighbours and places not to cross. There are still natives and lives that are nothing like yours. There is still the awareness that your stretching may be crushing those living invisibly under you. And as the ducks fly over, always the last to call it a day, it wonders when the night residents will come. It wishes it could stay to find out. It wishes it could stay. Root. Take it all in over centuries.

It stays. Flutters. A small scrunch. A mouse breath. Little beats of air. The briefest of contacts. It slips. As if into muslin: little pockets of air stitched tight; feeling itself splinter. There are breaks everywhere: tiny mouse-breaths, puncturing, rupturing. It feels strange to have a windpipe or lungs; such big bones, such large organs. Surely air comes in smaller than that. It becomes aware of its nostrils which seem about the right si ze. Perhaps it is a cluster of nostrils, flaring and shrinking; this seems more possible. Perhaps it is noss, and has no bones at all. This seems plausible. It waits for the mice to move over it. Little voles. Tiny paws. Hurried breathing. Mutters.

Stars come. From everything very small, to everything enlarged. Now it is longer than bones, wider than lungs, linear. If it has arms, they are only for pointing; if it has joints, they are stars; if it has legs, they are for leaping onto the next and the next. What it was before this is so pitiable it can barely remember it. It doesn't know how long it is a constellation or what brings it back. All it knows is returning, and walking once more along the grass, concerned once again with the moving over of ground.

But though it moves, part of it remains. The animal that lay in the earth, a star at its heart, tissue between the arms of its star, is what it is now. Free to roam but tethered, long and lithe beneath the badgers. Interlocking with the trees, mycorrhizal. The wax and wane of friendship in the dark; the give and take of hidden hosts. Beating and shining through the field to where he lies, the root of itself pulls up, forever trying to reach him.

32

X Absent

Swallows reel over, fizzing with early summer, as we wait. Summer is sooner each year, as seasons shuffle in the warming weather. When Nigel, the RSPB guide at West Town farm, arrives, the first birds he points out are house sparrows. He hears before he sees them. Looking up, we find a male singing from the eaves of a barn; higher still, out pops a female, without the black on the breast. There are about four couples in this area, he informs us, cocking his head in all four directions of sound. He talks about their habitat and eating preferences, breaking off now and then.

'I keep losing its thread,' he explains, 'because I keep hearing things.' As the walk progresses, this is what interests me most: how finely his hearing is attuned to the birds. 'I hear a song thrush,' he announces, though swallows and sparrows are the only birds in sight. 'Too far,' he mutters, before honing in instead on the collared doves that sit in the next field. 'They like being around humans,' he says, informing the group of their diet and how they like to eat the seeds off arable land.

He takes out an audio device and starts playing the sound of swallow song. Immediately one swoops across from where it has been nesting, flying so low over us that we see its breast feathers gleam. I wonder about luring it in with the promise of a potential friend or lover when all we have to offer is bodiless digital sound, when it already has so many new stimuli to contend with. Rising temperatures have meant that birds have had to adjust, with a number of species migrating earlier and changing their breeding patterns. Yet, not every species responds in the same way. Birds waiting in Africa for the changes in day length that will trigger their migration may find themselves arriving too late to catch the species they rely on for food, who may have been warmed into action sooner in England. It is a bewildering time to be a bird.

In the orchard we find a bright blue bird's egg in the grass. Nigel asks us what bird has come from it. No one knows. He runs through the different sizes of eggs for different-sized birds, showing us what a pheasant's egg looks like, a wood pigeon's. This, it transpires, is a song thrush's. 'Can you hear it?' he asks, but kindly, as if he knows it's beyond our human-tuned ears. 'It's at the top of the hill.' We pass through some scrubby woodland by the side of the old railway line, Nigel whispering 'goldcrest' to himself. 'I think it's further off, in that conifer,' he gestures to a tree, some distance away; it seems impossible that he could know what's in it. We wait while he plays his audio, and a tiny speck of bird floats down to a nearby branch. All eyes follow, landing on its golden head. 'It's my favourite bird,' a woman next to me breathes, pointing at a brooch on her lapel of a goldcrest. 'They tend to like conifers,' Nigel says, revealing how he had known where it would be.

Out into the open fields, filled with tall grass, we see swifts high in the air. Nigel explains how they live almost entirely on the wing, eating and sleeping as they go. They come from the Congo, he says.

'We've only recently learned new information about their route. We knew they came from the Congo, but now it seems they also go via Mozambique.'

'Why not just stay there?' Goldcrest woman asks.

And my mind drifts across the continents to Swahili, one of the languages of my mother. In Swahili there is no letter X. The sounds that this letter makes are entirely absent from the language. I think of the vocal alignments that exist because of this absence, that wouldn't be there with this other letter's presence. Sometimes, to hear one thing we must block out another. I think of the yellow focus that had brought my father daffodils and the spectrum colours of all his flowers since.

During the focus on birdsong, human sound diminishes, speech stalls. When conversation returns, it has moved on to consideration of how long birds live, with three or four years being the most common lifespan, if they make it past the perilous first year.

'But swifts average a few years longer,' Nigel says. We watch these long-living, sky-loving creatures float, just too far from us to be fully assimilated into knowing. Then, standing in the tall grass, Nigel pins his ears back. 'House martins,' he mutters, just as a group roams into view, circling over like little clouds. 'I'm just hearing wrens here,' he says, ears still pinned back, 'and a chaffinch over there – hear that single note? And, quite far off, a blackbird.' He moves through the grass, barely audible, 'I would have expected to hear skylarks.' A moment later he whispers, 'Hearing is the start of seeing.'

He tells us how Devon fields are good for attracting a variety of birds because they are often small, with mixed-enterprise usage.

'See that winter wheat,' he points up the hill, to the next farm. 'In areas like East Anglia you get field after field of that. Good for some species, but not others.' As we gaze over to the rippling green, his ears go back again. 'I'm hearing a distant skylark.' We wait. 'It will have nested over in that wheat,' he says. 'They nest in the tractor tracks but what's so threatening to them now is the timing of the agricultural processes. They need a solid two weeks for the eggs to be in the nest and a solid two weeks for the young to be in the nest. But if the tractors come back before that time, well then . . .' We all process the significance of tractor wheels over skylark nests. 'Being in the tracks like that, they're also prey to badgers, hedgehogs, foxes; anything that moves along the lines.'

A buzzard hovers into view.

'Would a buzzard eat a skylark?' someone asks.

'No, it would be too slow to catch it.' Relief is palpable through the group.

Back home, my legs and ankles throb. I think of the long grass we'd walked through and wonder if I've been bitten. My legs start to feel hollow, of unequal length. I feel them close over at the knees, at the pelvis; sense my joints more keenly, the body branching out in directions over which I have no control. I have felt what it is for stems to grow, low along and underground. But now they lift as they build, forcing the torso upwards. Parts of me spread wide: limbs scurrying under grass; others narrow: the straightening spine. Light moves up and down the luminous shift of the body.

As I enter my father's room, the light continues. There is far more than one small window can channel. It seems as though there were nothing but light, with little obstacles here and there, tiny objects. And in the light, sound carries like twigs of driftwood, bobbing up and down before lining up into speech.

'How was West Town?' he asks.

'OK.' When I had told him earlier where I was going, he'd said, 'What, to see a few sparrows?' which, of course, had been the first birds Nigel had shown us.

'I think it's a waste of time, this writing, isn't it?' he continues, getting right to the source of things as usual. I explain that it's not just History (which seems to be his main objection – 'History's dead!' he's assured me several times) but also Creative Writing: nature writing. I say that this has become a popular genre and he seems easier. We return to talk of birds: the magpie that nests in the chimney; the blackbird that flew straight into his room.

'It sings just here, below the window,' he says. 'There are so many of them.'

'It's a lovely sound,' I say. And, as if on cue, its distant ripple lilts through the room. I wonder how far off it is, and guess the hedge below. I long for ears as well tuned as Nigel's, that could probably stretch to the blackbirds that live out towards the copse, and wonder what it must be to live so fully in sound like that, so clearly hearing the notes that to others stay hidden.

'I suppose you get to know all the birds around here,' I say.

'Yes. Blackbirds are best, I think.'

'I agree.' We listen for a few more moments to the turn and tumble of its trills and I wonder whether Nigel can ever turn it off, this hidden language, or if the thread that he keeps losing ever snaps.

33

Xylophone

The first sounds are false starts. It strains its chords as no note comes. It is not used to this part of its mouth. It cocks its head. Though it is practised in listening, sound-making is a newer art. It tries again. Using the full arc of its mouth, its lips pull further apart than they have ever been. Its cheeks fill and fall, fill and fall, as the air pushes up from its throat. It is the very front of the mouth where sound gets syrupy. It has to forget what it has learned about using the stomach, the diaphragm, the full blast of the lungs. This sound comes from under the lips, from pinching the nose. It helps to smile.

Air hits the back of its teeth, its tongue becomes a hammer, its teeth a xylophone. Its cheeks inflate, hoarding sound like a squirrel. Tongue against teeth triggers a vibration. In xylophones, the shorter the bar that is struck, the higher the pitch. For a while it is a blackbird. Trill-la-la-lickwrrrrrrrrrrrrrrrrrrrrʳʳʳʳʳʳʳʳʳʳʳʳʳʳʳʳʳʳʳʳ Trill-lilla   liiiiirrwrrrrrrrrrrrrrrrrrrrrrʳʳʳʳʳʳʳʳʳʳʳʳʳʳʳʳʳʳʳwur- rwurrᵗʳⁱᶜᵏᵃˡⁱᶜᵏᵃˡⁱᶜᵏweowᶜʰⁱᵖᶜʰⁱᵖTrala-lilla. Then it pulls in its torso, thinning the sound, and is a robin. It pictures all its notes pinched in the middle. But it is the wren that seems most like itself. One trill into another at a speed too fast for the equipment in its mouth. But it tries: trptrptrptrptrptrpprrrrrrrrrrrrrrrrrrrrrrrrrrrrrrrrrrrrrrrrrr

prrrrrrrrrrrrrrrrrrrrr rrrrrrrrrrrrrrrrrrr^{tsweetsweeesweesweesweesweeeeee}
crrrrrrrrrrr^{tsweetsweeesweeswee}crrrrrrrrrrrrr up and down in
pitch as though hanging from a swing. This is the
kind of sound that is somewhere inside it. That shut-
tles up and down its vein. It recognizes the pulse and
tremor of it. It knows it has it in it.

And it has felt it before, this speeding sound. Back
in the winter, when its blades had beaten like wings
and its arms became strings as it had practised falling. It had heard it then, rising from the ground in
solicitude: shouldwecatchitshouldweholdit. The wind
had filled its bones, moving up and down the spaces
of the body, pooling at the joints, sounding at the
nodes. And the sound had filled with fir and moss,
eucalyptus and snowdrop; pushed up from, and along
into, grass. When the grass had spoken, it had felt
the words land inside itself; sound-maker and receiver
wondering what to make of each other.

Even before that, it had felt sound like this, lifting up from the soil. Curious, inquisitive, trying to
work it out: isithollowisitrungisitgrassorwomanisito-
neofussprungfromusorwhoisitwhatisit. Though this
was less like the touch of the air, over string or blade
or bar, and more the taste of it changing, like the fla-
voured flurry of a chemical reaction. Here the earth
had laid open, and as the grass had spoken it had
lifted up a soil singing with worms. Carrying their
signals with it, the grass's tinkling sound had drifted
over. It, too, was a familiar sound.

But to be sure of its own sound, it tries on some
other voices. The pigeon is too airy; it feels ridiculous
as it huffs and puffs the sound through. While the
pigeon inflates its chest, the Grassling uses the back
of its neck, the whole channel of its culm; air gushing

and wafting through the hole. What is it trying to say? There's no depth to it. The deep lowing of the cow from the next field is more substantial. This comes from the stomach and the bubble of the mouth, air taking up the whole head, which is frowning and limp. Sound pulls up from the pit, lolling around the head before tolling. Then it is a tractor. There is something soothing in the low sustained note, something freeing in the volume. But it can't quite get the tinny artificiality, the pang of notes hitting metal.

Then there is a fight in the hedge, it is all at the front of the mouth: peeppippypeeppippypippippip peeppippypeeppippypippippippp. Sparrows defending each branch. Here, the hammer on the bar is fast, the tongue on the back of the teeth unleashed with the furious swing of a gnat's wing. There does not seem enough time to match sound with touch and the voice inside it starts to rock with the thrill of it, recognizes the raucous spill of it. It wonders about the gnats, endlessly circling. It strains to hear and must get near. With its ear against them they bustle towards it, so their sound is ticklish, quick and lilting. Tseetsisstsisstsisstsisstsisstsiss tseetsisstsisstsisstsisstsisstsiss tseeeeeeeeeeeeeeeeeeeeeeeeee. The voice inside it is a little like this.

Then a gruff ruhhfff of a bark draws attention. It does not want to use a voice that way – roughly, pulling coarse against the chest like a knife up to the throat. Or too crudely. ARRGRRRRR ARRR ARRR ARRRR. The crow doesn't care who hears it. The fuss it makes. Leaning in with all its body, ruffling the whole length of it to make its point which puffs and paws the air it caws. The voice inside it is not like that. There are things to be said, but the whole field doesn't have to hear them. Or perhaps the whole field does hear them. And it feels, then, overwhelmingly, that that is exactly what a field is: millions of throats like this, millions of passages; channelling air and water and movement and things constantly touching and coming apart; it is all this, every blade of it.

34

Xylotomy

'Does it have a name, this book?' my father asks.

'Not yet,' I say. He frowns. 'Something to do with soil. Perhaps, *A Dictionary of the Soil*.' He frowns. 'No good?' He shrugs.

'Ask the blackbird.' A neighbourly blackbird is perched on the windowsill, looking in.

While xylology refers to the study of wood, xylotomy denotes the preparation of wood for study beneath a microscope. I feel cut open. That each page is fleshy and can't bear to be touched. Sunlight spills over the table beneath the window, leaving patches on the carpet. I follow the shallow pools: the black flight above, the white light below; the feeling of fast water rising. I hate to talk about the book before it is written. And to speak of it as a detached thing, that can be labelled, when it is a part of me, and of him – that makes the light curdle in my gut, sending chunks frothing along the throat until I cannot speak.

It is not his question I shirk from but those from outside the window, from outside the fields, outside of the space between us. Those that want to know what it is I am doing, where I am spending my time, what I am writing and why. I think again of William of Camden, that early topographer, answering, perhaps, only to the Society of Antiquaries, where he would meet with other influential topographers of the period – John Stow, Sir John Doddridge, Richard Carew – in Sir Robert Cotton's home, to share supper and discuss a scholarly paper. Where is the Society of Soil, Mourning and Metamorphosis, I wonder, where people who wander around fields slowly turning into something they don't recognize gather for lunch and read transcriptions of soil song?

Mark Brayshay says that Camden's work as a teacher enabled him to travel and work on his *Britannia* during vacations. I wonder how much he would get done if he was in this profession these days. I wonder if the light slipped along his neck like a tide rising. Perhaps it did. Perhaps it is inevitable, the beam that tracks you through the water. So invasive is the light that probes, that it is a wonder I do not choke and fall, here on the floorboards, or out on the street, to be gathered up by neighbours, asking what's wrong, and me saying *I don't want to talk about the book*, when I mean of course, *I want him to heal* and nothing more.

It begins to lose its value. It can feel like work to him too now, I know, at times. What was a welcome reaching to a shared place can now be the worry that he won't always be able to get there, or his fear that I'm spending too long in this place. And I start to fear it too. That it is taking too much from me, from us. That when the light recedes I will be stranded, a fish on the shore as the wildly lit waves crash into some other body; and what, after all, will be left? I leap and convulse at the barrenness. A shore without a sea. I look from the pool on the floor, across to him and back to me, standing still in the wrack, and throw my head back.

'Trilllalalick wrrrrrrrrrrrrrrrrrrr rrrrrrrrrrrrrrrrrrrrrrr Trilllillaliiiiirr wrrrrrrrrrrrrr rrrrr rrrrrrrrrrrrrrrrrrrr wurrwurr trickalickalick!' The blackbird starts, hops back a little, before flying off. And as we laugh, the sun trickles over us, the last of its evening light; not choking but stroking, as he is suddenly serious again.

'Well, but if it doesn't have a name, how should I think of it?'

'Think of it to do with soil. Think of it to do with Ide. Think of it to do with your work, your history, the family, and the fields.' He nods. It is enough. We are coming to understand each other.

35

Elk-sedge

itcomesitcomesitreallycomestousitsstemfoldsitscurvestouchourcurveit-strokespullsitsfingersthroughourhairfeelsthebristlesofourbladesfurof-flowersitfillswithuswemoveintoitsmouthitstoestenseitspillsitswordsin-toourswedouseitinlightbutonlyitseyesseeandtheymissmostofitbutthe-lightithasfindsitswayintoitsmouthandwhatcomesoutisachurningbutter-inglanguagetonguingdandelungingfromthegrasslingitnamesitswimmin-gthispullingofitselfoverthisflatteningtensings/wallowingitfeelsourwater-onitsskininitsthroatalongitswindpipeittinglesitsmouthopenswiderwepour-initexpandswhatisinitbesideswaterandbreathandwordsandlightitdoes-notseemtohaverootsyetthisfeelslikeonlythetipofititisheavy

As I move through the grass with her, it is strange to be talking to someone other than the land, or those living inside it. Blackthorn bursts in the Drewshill hedges as Rebecca, an artist, sketches. She talks about Cézanne. 'He was also interested in the depth of things, the extension beneath the ground,' she says. 'Are you concerned with the sky?' It's a startling question, and with the shamefaced-ness of someone realizing they've only been looking at half the picture, I reply that I am not. It's the ground level and deeper, beyond that, I say. Rebecca nods, as though this is a satisfactory answer, though I feel that it is not. After some time spent silently with the grass, I start making exploratory moves with my finger-tips. I press into the earth, slowly increasing the pressure. Is anyone in? Deeper fingers, then palms, rocking, kneading the ground. I take my socks off and the wet, soft grass – dandelion and clover – is delicious. I go through the same motions with my feet: first the toes, then the balls, then the rocking back and forth. This is the start, the sounding out, the seeing if the other is open to conversation.

'I'm about to roll,' I announce to Rebecca, who nods, securing our cameras. But the ground is full of water and I'm already starting to shiver, just from the contact of hands and feet. 'I'll wait for that cloud to pass,' I pronounce, as though it's of vital importance to the project, that I'm awaiting the perfect alignment of celestial and earthly bodies, but it is really just the small, all-too human need for warmth. As I hover between stillness and movement, nestling into wet grass, sedge, purple dead nettles, I hear the elk-sedge: a rune, depicting an 'x' sound in the Old English *Rune Poem*. Its flowering body calls from the ground, in amongst the grass it chinks and chimes, whispering its wetness. The light and water held on the grass-tips reminds me of my blade of grass, and home. Before I spin, I feel afraid of the wetness, of being out of control; of falling and not being able to stop. I feel fear of becoming field, of being swept into its contours. And what will I be when I roll over? A plough? That flattens the earth in order to mine it. But I won't take from it – only words. I won't penetrate – only soften. I let go.

Rebecca makes swift movements, dabbing and scratching the surface of the paper. And depth seems important to the paper too, to our movements over the recording material. I turn and turn into wetness. The plunge of it. The thud on the spine and the speed of it. Weightless. Unable to stop. Plummeting, grass on face, in ears, in throat. The hit of the spine. Were it not for that, I could go on forever. It is hard to stop. At the end I lie prostrate, face down, arms straight out in front. I must flatten in order to stop. Lying there, stretched and wet, I wonder if any of my ancestors lowered in this spot, this Druid's Hill, kneeling to this earth, in prayer. And I think of my father as I lie there: all body, all slippage. In the tissue of the land and skin and bone and sky, I think of him, across the fields. *He is still here*, I think, and I rise.

As I warm up from the wetness, things with wings visit. As if they see me more as one of them now, as a part of the field, or a type of tall grass. A cricket sits on the bottom of my jeans; a black beetle on my hand. A peacock butterfly brushes over my arm for the lightest of seconds. My arms glow. I start to think of my actions as a sort of poem:

FIELD SWIMMING
FIELD BATHING
FIELD STROKING

And just as with the water, I want to get back in. But I must be gentler on the spine that is already carrying an injury. So this time I roll sideways, a horizontal, rather than vertical turn. Arms and legs stretched, as long as I get, I come to the top of the hill and tip. At the start, the eye is a camera. Blades of grass in the foreground, landscape correcting itself in the back, to form a picture. I try to keep my eyes open, though they keep wanting to close. I want to record everything. Be fully in the moment, yet also to store it. I let go. The same phrase from my earlier action. What is it that I am letting go, when I fling or slip along a landscape? The responsibility of standing up? It is a casual disappearance, this exit from gravity. An absence that can be readily achieved, that I can fit into dailyness.

As I move, I find I am rotating into the direction of the hedge, instead of straight down the hill. Once more, it is difficult to stop. I pause on all fours and wait for the world to stop spinning, and when it seems to, jump up. But no sooner am I standing than I plummet three, four, five steps down again. The hill is still in me – its incline, its roll. Finally, I come back up and try again. I will myself to remain in a straight line but this requires so much tension in the body that I give up and allow myself to roll where I want to – back towards the hedge. My angle is taking me parallel to the church below, in the valley. I wonder about the possibility of some sort of spiritual ley line.

And here, in land, the body regulates your possibilities, just as in the sea. When the coldness of the water dictates the duration of the movement, here it is the coldness of the wetness of the grass. And if you lived beyond that? In the soil? Are you still subject to the body's limits? I wonder about the temperature of the soil, and how the worms weather it. In cold spells, they burrow down more deeply. They can even freeze entirely, then be thawed back to life. I think about the tiny resurrections that may be taking place under me, in the warming soil.

A fly moves along a blade, close by. It has legs *and* wings, which seems greedy. Though it walks along the grass, at any moment it could lift itself off and into air. It edges along the edge of things – all leg. I try it for a while, taking a long, slow stalk through the grass. As I walk into the hill's incline, I approach its brow. Where does the field become a hill? Where does the head become the spine? Where is the neck of the hill? Flat becomes curved, spine ricochets into ribs, erupts into breast. I stroke the field, pulling fingers through grass like hair: the soft clover, spider, beetles; the small button mushrooms, the open dandelions. Breast. Stroke. I start field swimming. Again, words come as poems:

BREAST STROKING
NETTLING
DANDELUNGING
GRASSLING

Pulling my fingers through, my mouth fills with grass, my toes dig in to propel me. I feel my internal circuitry change: I am plant as well as animal. My blood transports oxygen; my chlorophyll produces it. Oxygen, carbon, hydrogen, nitrogen, phosphorus surge along tissue, torso, culm, to my blades. Blood blends magnesium as well as iron. I am grass made flesh. Grassling.

With no malleable water to move through, only fixed ground, I have to use my body more. The push comes from the toes, which are rooted, along my culm to the knees, which repeat the movement, only larger and deeper. Leaved arms sweep out, gathering and spreading wetness and sweetness; the words get tangled: swetness and spreetness; weading and sweeting; all knotting and breathing in and over the tongue.

Once more, I knead the earth, wondering about its energies. How churches were dowsed and located on ley lines of supposedly beneficial energies. If the land, like the body, can hold a trauma (I think of where he lies, across the fields), it can also, perhaps, hold a healing. I always feel better here, always. When I pull up from the field, it is as if from a spa. Skin tingles with life. I breathe it all in, the moment, and the capture of the moment. The moment where I am closer to my father through being in a space that he has been in. A space where his father has been, and his father too. And I will tell him about the field, though not the rolling and spinning and swimming, but I needed all that to get in. To get close enough to what is here; to what it feels and means to be here. By being here, I become part of his story. Through a shared space and shared narrative, I write myself into him.

36

Yeanling

When I next come to rest, I am surrounded by buzzing things. Their noise and movement seem overwhelming and it is difficult to comprehend so much life in one small space. Light panicles of grass dangle against my lips. In my mouth is something small, hard and round which I suck on; it has the bitter twist of a peppercorn. I lift my head and look left towards the dark woods, then pan right across the burnt scalp of field my father's map calls Brake. Beyond that, the open ploughed soil of Lankham. Up close, the glistening heads of sweet vernal-grass.

I shift my legs beneath me, sitting inside my father's map. The sketch of field boundaries and names, long pored over from a distance, has come to life. A map is a layer of space, but never its force. But now that force is here, and I am part of it. I think of the functions of mapping. If a map is used to prevent you from getting lost, then what do you need when you come to get lost? Or when you come in order to move into the past and into the present combined. When you come to listen to those living there now and also those hidden, below the soil. When you come to listen to them and to live like them, briefly, to roll and to stretch and to stride and to burrow. When you come to do all that presentness, but at the same time to go backwards, into what was here before. When you come to go present and backwards and slant. As you imagine and join, and allow words to bring a conclusion to what before was possibility. What kind of a map do you need for that?

I think it might still bear the outlines of things. Field boundaries, roads. But within that, how would it capture time? The multiplicity and porousness of the life in the place? And if it did, somehow, manage it, how could it update, rather than staying static? Could there be a way, through brush strokes? Grass strokes? Words? Through both Rebecca's approach and my own, together? Swetness and spreetness, weading and sweeting, knotting and breathing in the burnished grass.

The field is a swathe of leaf, only the vernal-grass approaching flower. We wade through, back towards the village, as bright bursts of peacocks, orange-tips, tortoise-shells and commas flit through. We are closely pursued by two horses, breathing heavily at our necks – a supernatural presence. The bank ahead has a covering of lamb's-ear, its foliage lying under hair so woolly that it looks like a lamb. I remember the one that gambolled a few fields from here, near Markham Cross, trying out its new body. I had envied its willingness to strike out alone on legs it had never known before, carrying its unprecedented load. A lamb, or yeanling, starts to walk soon after birth, only taking nutrients from its mother's milk for a few months before it can get all it needs from grazing. And though I am closer now to grass, have tasted its peppery leaves and chewed the blades, have felt my own skin become a different thing, splitting open into leaf, I do not feel independent. I feel connected still, by a root, by a thread, to where my father lies. I gather up the soft green strands of lamb's-ear to take to him.

I leave Rebecca at the Huntsman Inn where her taxi pulls in, and walk back up the hill. Passing close by the fields I had seen before from a distance, I notice how Lankham field's soil has been churned; open and wounded yet not necessarily hurting. For humans, to be that exposed evokes pain: a cut, a rupture, but perhaps it might also be a release. A turning out of what has been in, like speech.

I look at the speech of the field. A lunar landscape, with great chunks of hardened earth rising in boulders beside cut channels where the plough has dug deep. This is the pause in a conversation that is waiting for a reply. These are the sentences, lined along the ground, hoping to be heard. Here is a bank of memories, pulled from the back of the land. There is a hesitancy in their shape, in the space they occupy, the empty furrows. These rows could be an entry-point for the past and for all kinds of present. A vulnerable, intimate opening to the world which might not be painful, but may just be workable, that could even be a perpetual way of being.

I answer the soil. Belly down, along a furrow. Arms forward. Ground is deep, hard and punchy. Tough, like cement cracked open. As I swim, I inhale manure. Flies gather. I have limited movement, as the soil is too stiff to break. As my fingers push against it, a slight crumbling gives a little, but the huge, hard channels are largely immovable. It is like swimming through rock. None of the pleasure of the wet open grass; here the soil is a straitjacket. How can I answer such hardness?

I start to panic as I stretch and turn; the furrow becomes a coffin and the flies intensify. I know there are things the earth holds that I do not want to face. I had felt this by the pond near the withy beds. I had felt this in the mulch and the rot and the swallow of mite and beetle and snail. I had known this when the leaf had let go of its lignin rib and the fungi spread across its tip. I had even known this when I met the buck who would lose its antlers, who would feel them harden and the blood flow through the velvet membrane until it peeled away and they fell to the ground, shrouded in moonlight, waiting to be found. But I am not ready to find them. I raise myself up and out to the side, just as a car swipes past. I move unsteadily, as if I am new to feet. My whole body stained with earth, trailing its dusted afterbirth.

SOIL MEMOIR FOR TEN ACRE FIELD

Horizons:
ins.
0–9
A

9–14
(B)

14–24
(B) /C

24+
C

What would you tell the you that was here before this? Or the one here before that? Would you tell it that grief would break from its head like a bird from its shell. That its body would stop, feet buckle, legs cave; that here, in the grass, would be its ending? That cries like squeaks would draw out from it, long and coarse, to creak the air as bows against tight strings. That its gasps would shake the wind which would hurl itself through its leaves, leaving it bent and trammelled. That it would moan. Sustained notes from its belly: pure pain. That air would gutter down its bone. That when it had thought it had found a way to go on, it hadn't. Or would you say nothing. So that this broken moment, this severance, would cut this cleanly; no hope, no body, no love ever as great as this loss.

37

Yeomen

My great-grandfather, William Archer, was born at Sheldon: a working farm, before it was sold. And the land there has a kind of magnetic pull over me. I had felt it as a child, when I had visited; and again, the last time in Ten Acre field, before I had known of any family connection. I feel it now, where the fields flow and fold above the Teign. I walk down the hill to the village of Christow, where the church holds a cluster of Archer graves. What had caused this family to grow here?

My father says the Archers from Poitou in France helped William the Conqueror win the Battle of Hastings in 1066 and that their names are inscribed upon the Battle Abbey Roll. They were rewarded with land in England. One branch of the Archer family was given large estates in Cornwall by William in the Lizard, and can be found in the records as 'an ancient and honourable race'. But my father has always been more concerned with the humbler branches of the family: the yeomen. He explains how yeomen grew up from around the thirteenth century when towns and industry developed. Since these workers had little opportunity to grow their own produce, yeomen emerged as a group who devoted their lives to growing food, not simply for themselves but to sell to others for profit.

He reveals how some Archers moved eastwards from Cornwall into Devon in the Middle Ages, but warns that it's impossible to establish exactly when the family arrived in Christow: *the parish records begin in 1558 but the first pages are almost illegible.* The International Genealogical Index shows concentrations of

Archers in the Middle Ages on the estates of the Pomeroy family. *Oddly enough, if we look at the map, Berry Pomeroy to Christow, through Highweek and Ilsington, is a dead straight line.* So this has preoccupied him as it has me, this mapping of human over landscape, this interplay of person and place. As my roots have let me travel further down into earth, I have begun to feel that the line may, in fact, begin below the surface, that it may be geological. Some fault line where the earth cracked and something other than human dictated that this family form a life here. I feel the older and deeper periods of movement – the earth's – beneath all the human life that surfaces. I reach.

As we have seen, many Archer families, once so ubiquitous in Devon, have in the twentieth century died out. The social group they once belonged to, their habits and way of life, have disappeared with them, and the yeomen of England will probably in a few years from now be totally extinct. I think of the farming family I visited near Dartmoor; others at Morchard Bishop and in Cornwall; and one, only one, still in Christow. And I know the place began before them, and will continue afterwards. Yet this family has had an impact on the land as it has had on them: their farming for miles around, their care of what was in and on the soil for generations.

My father talks about the particular beliefs and responsibilities belonging to the yeomen. *In addition to their work as farmers, members of the family through the ages, starting with Edward in the middle of the seventeenth century at Christow . . . played their part in local government, constituting, in fact, a conscientious and unpaid civil service.* Principled and independent, these old farming families have given, as they have taken, from the soil. *To do this they had to have land, they had to be paid a fair price for their produce and, above all, they had to be left free to farm in their own way.* If we are witnessing a time when the care of the land passes from families to corporations, with very different guiding principles, then does it reach too far to say the small personal loss of a family could be a large-scale loss for the planet?

From the churchyard, I walk past Sea Hill, the house where my grandmother grew up. This grandmother's father was born at Sheldon, while her husband, Wallace Burnett, came from Ide. I feel the forces that fold a family together along the earth. Could there be foundations in people – undercurrents, fault lines that connect them – that work to bring them together? The Bridford Thrust, which passes through the railway cutting near Sheldon and reaches on to Idestone, was created during the mountain-building phase at the end of the Carboniferous period. Rock formations from the south moved slowly over existing rock on a fault dipping to the south at a shallow angle.

The earth has brought us together before, I think, as I circle back to Sheldon past the railway cutting. Placing one foot carefully before another, I wonder how long it would take me to reach him. If I kept walking now, one foot before the other – five hours? I close my eyes, one foot before the other. Five centuries? Millennia? The years line up, one era before the other. Will the earth keep us, if I ask it (one word carefully before another), together?

38

Ymbclyccan

I wake to the blackbirds in the small of the morning. A thin strip of blue just above the hill, then apricot, then lemon, then blue again. Mist swirls over the fields, making a sea between land and sky. My culm is tender from field swimming, lungs tight from soil swimming. I still feel the dust along my windpipe. When I look at my arms I notice raised rivulets; the soil has imprinted me with a second set of veins, of bones, like an exoskeleton. I try to unknot but it's too painful: my spine is bunched up and over like gnarled branches of an ancient oak. I trace the hills of the body: behind the neck, the small of the back, buttock into leg, the quarry of the navel. With my hair up and baked browner from the sun, I look just like a hare and wouldn't look out of place popping out from a hedge.

I have always wanted to sit in a hedge. The overlooked passageways between field and road that buzz and bulge with hidden life. The rabbits popping in and out, the scurrying bank voles and harvest mice, the flutter and call of bursts of birds. In the Ide hedges, I think of the long-tailed tits with their electronic beats, the silent speech stirrings of bats. The sense of age a hedge brings, having been here, some of them, since the Bronze age, when ancient farmers cleared the woodland, leaving strips as boundary lines. Now the sight of a very long hedgeline may indicate such age. Though it can be difficult to date these to the Bronze era, many of these long Devon hedgelines have been traced to the Anglo-Saxon, when some landowners were simply confirming the boundaries of existing Celtic settlements. I am at home within these Celtic boundaries, with my strong affinity with the Druid's hills. But the pull back even further, to a Bronze era when the areas of land under cultivation expanded, adds a new intensity.

Through the slow lifting night, a hedge starts chattering. Not with the patter of birds, but of water. I swipe sticky weeds away to find a pool, gathered inside, and out from it, a running stream. Needing enough force to break through bramble and nettle, yet holding the body steady enough so as not to cannon into the pool, I advance. I meet darkness, but with a slight light dappled through the breaks in the branches and glinting off the ground-water. I crouch, not wanting to disturb the floor. As the sun grows, more lives begin to take shape. What had looked, at first light, like nettles, are the heart-shaped leaves of garlic mustard, or Jack-by-the-hedge. Its white petals begin to shine, while heads of cow parsley glint higher up, and a shimmer of blue builds as bluebells come into focus. I pull the blue into my palm, breaking a little off; a few bright bells to take to him.

To be classed ancient, these hedgerows only have to have existed before the Enclosure Acts of the eighteenth century, and to be considered species-rich, contain five native woody species, or be rich in herbaceous plants. I wonder how many humans have been logged inside a hedgerow. But even here, in this tiny hideaway, are threats. The pesticides used in the fields are seeping in, threatening the wildlife and plants within. Cases have been charted of bees consuming pollen from neonicotinoid-treated crops and wild flowers, ingesting lethal doses of fungicides and insecticides.

I curl inside the trees, inside the word the hedgerow breathes: *ymbclyccan*, from the Old English word meaning 'to surround or enclose', 'to encircle or embrace'. It is a lovely word to hold inside a face. I let it roll around my mouth, behind my teeth, and into air; and once it's there it trickles down along the limbs, all earthward-bound. Its circle is a sound so round, *ymbclyccan* all the grassy ground.

I unfurl from my hedge-held form. Roll my head around the pivot of the neck, let my leaves sweep out wide, circle; smoothing the air, spreading myself out flat. Sun pours through my shoulder blades, pushing them back and down. Spaces grow around the neck, between the toes. Every gap in and between the body has potential. Here are the soft parts of myself that will grow if I let them. If I make enough space and protect it. Flowers do not come from strong, open poses. They come in the small, protected bulbs of the body. They grow in me like a silent radiance.

And as I look across the wide expanse of field and hill, out to the shine of the Exe and the distant sea, I think about the language of this place, of myself, and how I must keep it open. How I must stay out, out in grass voice, in field voice, in open-throated hill voice. 'Soil voice' is a cough. A release. A cough-it-all-up, get-it-all-out, with a widening of the throat, a glottal opening, into chasmic voice: an outburst! An ungovernable quake of a voice; vowels shaped into an eruption of e's and h's, into a stream of 'ehhhh' as in the breath of the earth, as in the coughing up of clumps, of fur balls of blackthorn, of blackbirds, of history, of mourning, of hope, of new mornings; of all this the soil sings – of all that has been held in.

39

Ymbgedelf

Since the mapping and drawing, rolling and swimming, I have been feeling, in some way, like a living map. An evolving, human sketch of my father's pencil sketch, which I now long to feel physically. My father's sketch was based on the 1803 survey map of the manor located in the cathedral archives. When I get there, I am admitted by a suspicious woman who informs me that you usually need to make an appointment.

'Got a young girl here,' I hear her explaining from behind the door ('young girl!'). The archivist comes out, immediately welcoming, and within a couple of minutes has brought me what I need. In fact, she has brought two books. But I'm puzzled to find no map in either. Some further investigation shows that the archivist has brought item 68C rather than 86C, and I wonder if it is my father, or the archive, that has made the transcription error. The second of the books seems to have the right title, *Manor of Ide, Survey by Alexander Law*, the closing words to which, '*with Map*', leap loudly.

'Where do you suppose the map is?' I ask, nonchalantly, masking palpitations.

'That's strange, I'll have another look. What exactly are you looking at, in Ide?' I have no way of answering her. She returns in a few minutes, saying she is having trouble finding it.

'Are you local?' she asks, by way of ascertaining whether it will be possible to come back another day if it can't be found today – again, with no idea of how large a question this is, how impossible to answer. As I wait for her return, I look at the books in front of me. The one that is not a survey is the *Book of Court Rolls*. It contains page after page of references to Ideites' dealings with the court: money due in 'homage'; licences granted. On one page is a table entitled 'Lands in the parish of Ide in the County of Devon'. It contains a small list of names, some now familiar – 'Drakes Meadow'; others not – 'Over Meadows', 'Path Meadows'. A 'Cultivation' column gives insight into land use: 'arable' for one, 'orchard' or 'meadow' for others.

I scrunch my eyes to decipher new fragments of writing, thinking how much of the work of a historian must be deciphering handwriting. The book varies widely in neatness; some sections are entirely illegible, so that it is like a cool stream when you come across the neatness of others. On some pages, the author has copied out again what was previously written, as if to show that they realized it was illegible. I wonder if it is the same author or a later one. I find myself imagining the life of whoever it was who wrote so messily, who scratched out whole pages in frustration, even cutting off the end of one page completely, as though sawn. Handling the heavy paper, the ink scratched in laboriously, saying something of the writer's moods where things have been blocked out, I think about how these elements have been lost in electronic writing. The writer's mood, personality; whether they are in a hurry, or cold, or at ease. And I think of Rebecca, scratching paint into – not just onto – the page. How does that depth and layering get into the digital? Even if you use a digital pen to write, or scan in your handwriting, or layer typescript like a concrete typewriter poem, it's all artifice, not necessity, as computers offer page upon page of uniform boredom.

And we sit. Three women in a room, poring over old paper, muttering dates. The odd triumph, smile, involuntary burst; but, more often, a steady, monotonous mining. Centuries-old ink lifting up from pages as our fingers probe – *ymbgedelf* or 'digging around'– the tattered corners of the past. The frequent inscrutability of the ink reminds me of the sixteenth-century parish records my father described as *almost illegible*, unable to reveal the family names that may have rested there. What power writing has to mark a history. The woman who had reluctantly admitted me has mellowed now it is apparent that I too am involved in 'serious work'. She smiles at me in between muttering. An older lady sits behind them in the sun. I wonder what she is working on. I wonder how it is written. I shift in my seat and feel colour come, from the flowers deep inside me. They will be a different texture to my own, thinner and more precarious. They will uncurl and stretch into space and I will have to move with them to release them. I feel this, as I sidle more fully into sun.

40

Ymbwendung

In the soft pull of petals, the scent is sweet. If you let it in, the sweetness travels deep along the nostrils, the throat, the windpipe, the culm, the lungs, the leaves. The mellow breeze laps the flowers' lips open to lime stigmas, powdered in pollen. The honesty's petals are white near the centre, lighter pink further out, and lined with purple veins, though most would simply call the flower purple.

My first second in the honesty, I grow accustomed to colour: the different shades that humans reduce to one. The purple depths, flecked with green and white and pink, pull in the body until it sinks. I flounder in the silky sway of flowered foam and freshening spray. The head is caught. It hangs from my neck like a jewel. It glints in the speckled water. The flower's Latin name, *lunaria*, means moon-like. The seed pods that develop after the flowers have dropped are white, round and lunar. But these are not here yet. The head is not a moon that steers the tide, but a stone that drops in purple light.

In the next second, I come to see all those I share the flowers with. Wasps, hoverflies, aphids. All manner of winged things I still do not have the names for. I try to store their images like figures in a line-up. To remember their shade and sound and shape. But I am pummelled by their movement. Their tiny flapping seems so far removed from flying. That a soaring upward drifting might need this small repeated lifting, this furious fling of wing is perplexing. There is an endless rushing and beating, a perpetual bringing together of parts, like a door that won't swing shut – but just for a moment it does – and the smallest touch is enough to make it all worth it; all the running and beating and rushing and the fleetingness of it.

Next, I notice other plants: the sticky willow, stinging nettles, forget-me-nots. The last come as a shock. It is startling to find a whole stretch of blue has been obscured by the purple. I notice this as you do a face that strikes you in a crowd, not of anybody you know, but of something you have shared, a face that shows the signs of a sorrow you know. Though it is a cheerful flower, with the speckled blue chintz of a school summer uniform, still it says to you, *Don't forget me*, and I feel, all at once, like crying. I think of the first clutch of this flower I took to him, of the sky they made of his room. But only for a moment because that is just one of the notes in the purple that is thick and leaved and light and gloved and this purple is a purple that I love.

Now I register birds. Their song flows into the petals whose strokes are smooth as seaweed and the first is a robin, ^{tseeptseep chip} chippychippytsippychippychippy ^{chuppachuppachuppa} then it is a wren: trptrptrptrptrptrp_{rrrrrrrrrrrrrrrrrrrrrrrrrrrrrrrrrrrrrrrrrrrprrrrrrrrrrrrrrrrrrrrrrrrrrrrrr} rrrrrrr_{tsweetsweeesweesweesweesweeeee}crrrrrrrrrr ^{tsweetsweeesweeswee}crrrrrrrrrrrr Then sparrows and long-tailed tits. Their notes cup its face, drawing it right up to them; notes as gentle, probing, as fingers.

Then, as I fall forward into flower, I feel only fear. Only the dread of being separate from the ground is real to me now. Though I know the earth is not far, a fall is still a fall, no matter the distance. I feel my tongue poised in my mouth, breath leaps, everything readying for the scream. But my hands find the ground and chest falls as the sweetness takes over everything. *Ymbwendung*, 'reviving', is a word smothered in this flower. This: the flower my father had brought from his field to the hospital on the day of my birth. This: the colour that had greeted me, the smell, the taste, the soft landing.

And so my heart flips whenever I come upon honesty, as I do now, looking up from my book, glimpsed through the library window. This is the rush that comes, the purple flood, the longing. And, this time, the rest of my body has to follow. I must pull into the flight of the bee, whose own map is rich, stitched strict into spatial memory. I must fly straight and quick, out of the room, into the tossing of petals, the surge and sway of fluttered surface. Letting my chest rise and fall, rise and fall, into the rhythm of the flower's call, something flows. Something comes to rest. Colour floods into scent. Notes of mown grass and vanilla; lavender, clover, cherry. Apricot and strawberry drift and warm. The bee's path draws me in, as I summon a strength I have been building. With a long exhale, my flowers join the air: the *tseep* of birds, the sweep of clouds, the back and forth of sunlit hours; they are part of this now, until the end.

The sweetness deepens. Tobacco and aldehydes lay a masculine note inside vanilla. To flower is to father as well as mother. And if he has a scent, it is this. The bass note in the coumarin coming from me. The woodiness in the sweet vernal-grass. The steel of a fork, of a spade. The crumble of earth across blade. The checked cotton shirt, the tweed jacket, rubber boot. The suede safari shoe. The pressed trouser, the vegetable root. The army knife and the twine, the paper and leather spines. All of these mingle and merge in the bright purple verge.

In sweet vernal-grass, the change from vegetative tip to young inflorescence is so quick that scientists have found it difficult to study, though they feel it must be there. They think that something does not become something else without leaving signs. But I know it can be instant. The change the honesty makes in me is immediate, as I sink into the slick of its scent, trailing bees. At dawn and dusk I repeat my release, in the bursts of time when sweetness over-powers. For seven days I breathe out flowers.

When I pick myself up, I look back at the dent I have made. Carefully, I take each flattened plant by the stem, coaxing it back to its original position. I am glad not to have left much of an impression. Moss gleams from beneath like coral at the base of the sea floor. As I move off and back inside, freshened by petalled water, I pick at my hair, finding little purple shreds. I shed bright strands along the ground; white filaments spray my head with a premature ageing.

41

Yr

When the map arrives, it is stunning. The mellowed admittance woman gasps, bending over it. I feel irrationally proud, like I've given birth to it: yes, here it is, the map I have summoned from the archives! Its glamour comes from a gold line snaked across it. The fact that it is in colour comes as a surprise. There is no key, so I'm not sure what everything represents, but the gold indicates some sort of boundary line. There are also two shades of green, blue, red and orange. In some places, one colour has been placed over another, producing new ones, like red and blue emerging purple. I think back to what Rebecca said about mixing colours and look at the Drewshill fields. They are bounded in green, which makes me smile, as it is this green that had sung out to us too, in words as well as paint, when we were there.

I find that my father has worked out the key, so I don't have to. In his Sketch Map No. 3, he has added a 'Key to Symbols used' which shows how the different letters in the fields correspond to different farms. 'R' indicates fields belonging to Pynes farm, and I can see where the footpath from the Drewshill fields now emerges. The fields labelled with a 'Y' are too far left to feature in my father's map. For the first time I realize that he too had a specific area of focus, as I have with the Drewshill fields. For him, it is very much the eastern side of the village – around what used to be Woolmans farm. The map as a whole is much larger than the section that he has used. I take a photo of the section that corresponds with his, wondering more about his own boundaries.

To find the section he used for Sketch Map No. 2, I have to navigate my way by looking at the buildings. I look for the same shapes that appear on his map. Like a game of Tetris, I see how shapes might fit together from one map to the other. It takes a long time, as the survey map operates on a different scale and I have to keep making spatial adjustments. As I trace the Tetris pieces together, I fall on some writing: 'Part of the Estate called Great Marshall, the Property of Mr Edward Smallridge', and it reinforces what my father writes about this land being parcels belonging to particular people, strongholds; perhaps, in places, 'pockets of Romano-British settlement' surviving long after the Anglo-Saxon conquest. There are also interlocking parish boundaries. Clockwise, the parishes go – Alphington, Exminster, Dunchideock, Ide, so that when you say the name of a place, it is difficult to know what you mean because it is always a collection of other places too – and of people, and of powers. A gathering of state, of local authorities, and, as I glance back at the *Book of Court Rolls*, of Church. Collectives and individuals, dominion and resistance, all bound together in one earth.

It is good seeing the map spread out like this, though I am self-conscious about gazing at the map for as long as I am. Do the fields it shows know what a power they had? What a force to have drawn me to them. To have drawn my father and his and his. Is it sacred? Is it the accidental circumstance of being somewhere that offered work to my great-grandfather, or is it more than this? The Anglo-Saxon rune *Yr* depicts a bow made from a yew tree. This rune denotes the perfect application of skills and knowledge to natural materials. This rune lets you know when you are in the right place. Is the map this kind of rune? That, it doesn't say, though I ask it. The archivist sits opposite and I don't know what she must think of my protracted pauses, seemingly staring into nothingness. But there is so much that this map is telling me.

It tells me about the parts of Ide that were important to my father: Woolmans and Great Marshall. It tells me about the colours of the fields. It shows me who the people were who lived in these places, and the names that have held on. It shows how authorities, governmental and religious, trace their own maps over the land, over people's homes, and names, drawing boundary lines on the shore for time's tide to wash away or bring back, as if by whim, years later. It also shows that maps have long been a source of aesthetic pleasure; that someone, centuries ago, felt that this one merited a gold line, a red, a green; not knowing that over two hundred years later it would cause an old woman to gasp and a younger one to smirk like a beatific mother. And so, in its own way, it tells me to go on making things of beauty, and, though my literary head shouts 'don't use the word beauty', I shout it down this time. It's the right word for this gold line, for this crumpled, centuries-old paper; for this tiny, tactile memory.

42

Yslende

A golden field, just above a Woolmans field, is caught in the middle of a fold. The map has been folded into twenty small squares and this field lies in the bottom left corner of the top right square. You have to look deep into the fold to see what is there; it has been literally pressed down, so that a human hand has buried the land into the crevices of paper. You almost need to walk into the map to find it; to get out guy ropes and tack down the rugged paper. The pinch of where the corners meet is intimate, like the pistil of a flower, a small, private part. My eyes flick across to the Drewshill fields, wrapped in their green border, with flecks of gold above and beneath: top left and bottom left. I do not move. Swollen with sap, a great pressure builds in my head.

Here the land speaks through paper, weathered by centuries of waiting. But words have been pushing up all over the place lately: from soil, from wood, from stone; from all manner and matter of buried time. Records of earlier touchings of hand and earth; Old English tongues, Anglo-Saxon runes, are surfacing. I twist, dusted in gold, as the word *yslende* covers my lips. Glowing. My tongue has to feel its way into the word, like a bee to a flower, then out again, as the last push of its sound is whispered. *Yslende* glows the golden field, *yslende* all along the fold, *yslende* in between the hills. My petals pull apart. I spill.

I am lying still in the wheat. Sun washes over – scurrying at the base, floating over the top. This is a day that is to come or, perhaps, has already been. I feel the ripening of skin and lightening of hair. My stem is supported by the soil, the churning molten core, massaging the spine, releasing the nodes. Webs of rain spin on my tips, dots of water glitter the changeling water. Sounds rise. A swallow. A swoop. A swallowing, swooping root. Layered in the hay, in the tightly bounded day, lightly woven. A netting barely visible: the skin starts to itch with each twitch of wheat.

Clover skin is tightly bound in pollen gusts, seeded dust, bursts of swallow in the hay swallowed swover. Words mix and swoop in the swalloving sway. My eyelids flutter. I swoon in the heat in the heart of a day in midsummer. But my own growth has passed the middle; I am a long way into turning into something else: from animal to grass, from grass to hay, from summer to a saved day. I recognize this feeling, of having been saved at the right time, before the rain, sun still seeping in through its lids. To be brought out again, perhaps, in winter and swallowed thick and still turning, still burning, with lives inside, the scent and the shape and the colour bursting and thirsting, swalloving, swovering, wooping and swooping. And the smell is what matters here. The pull of the sweetness in the grass, dairy sweet, nestling sweet, suntrap sweet; the scent and the sweep. The inside so sweet: the seeds.

And as I splatter into soil I soak in and down the buried language of the ground. I seep into the marrow of the bones of the land. And I call as I fall – to rock, a faint cuckoo, a last halloo. Everything responds, everything is on: listening and being heard are simultaneous. The sounds of becoming and belonging are the same as the spaces opened up for them. My body hollows and braces in the flood of the quiet places.

I enter the earth and speak with the tongues of birds, of worms, with latticed roots, all along my fibres and fathers and mothers and grasses; I rain speech. Itisoccupiedwithsoundandhowtopressitinto-somethingflatitcarrieswithititssoundisallaboutanotheritnamesfather-hetolditaboutthisplaceitsmappedearthedsongbeatshhhhhhhhhhhh-hhhhhhhhhhhhpillowhhhhhhhhhh

glow.   (gold. willow.)
shhhhhhhhhhhhhhhhhhhhhhhhhhhhhhhhhhhhhhhhhhhhhhhhhhhhhhhPILLOW

wehearitquickandsmallinthesoilithitsrootsandstonesthatgrindbeside-
itlingeringonshalethroughrockitthumpsanddropsitssharpnesspicking-
fernoakbeechstrippeditpressesintosoilliftingsaltfromdeepoceanall-
thewaybackupmillionsofparticlesofclayofsiltupthroughmillionsof-
bacteriathereachofitfromheartobeatingheart.

I blink. The field moves back to wherever it has been, no longer bound by gold but green. I start to question what I've seen, where the map has taken me. Perhaps to a folded-over moment in history that had needed to be opened. Perhaps to an earlier dream where I had seen the fields hemmed by a border made of water. Then, I had entered the stream and swum until it swelled into a pool. Now, I had entered the paper's knot until it flattened into a sea of dew and a space that grew to a soft cuckoo. Or perhaps it was a moment that was yet to come, that here, resting on the tip of summer, I had only sensed approaching.

All I really know is that soon the map will close. And I will walk out into the city, showering my pollen, scattered by the wind. And the archivist will carry on cataloguing and the map will be covered and returned to its shelf, perhaps for another two hundred years. But I am happy it's there. Glowing its hidden gold from behind its cloth and wooden box. I'm glad it's there.

43

Ȳtemest

'How long are you staying this time?' he asks, the day that I am leaving. But time has started running differently here. He is a mountain, and has millions of years; I am still not sure what I am, but know that it is something thin and long and stretched out. Something that can be here and yet not here. In his room, yet out in his acre. In his acre, yet out in Druid's Hill. In Druid's Hill, yet out in Ten Acre Field. It is only when I am in a distant city that I lose my elasticity. That I can't seem to hold all the places together.

So although part of me wants to say, 'Forever' and mean it, it doesn't really matter what I answer. I could say what we have: minutes; or I could say what we really have: hundreds of millions of years. 'Ȳtemest,' is what I actually say. He waits. 'Uttermost. To the uttermost ends of time,' I whisper, as the blackbird flies into the window, landing with a boom against the glass.

'Back again!' he smiles.

'Back again!' I smile. And I want to sing in the blackbird's voice, the way I have learned to now. But the sound won't come. Out at the uttermost, the extreme edge of our time together, there is not enough breath for song. Here, the lower air pressure makes it difficult for oxygen to enter our blood. Normal physical activities become impaired: climbing the stairs, thinking clearly, recalling memories. Perhaps it is this oxygen deprivation that has plagued him, where doctors attribute other kinds of ailments. Perhaps it is this that worries me. When we travel to high altitudes, our bodies initially respond inefficiently, straining our breathing and as much as doubling the heart rate.

The severity of altitude sickness may be due, in part, to your genes. Indigenous communities in the high Andes valleys in Bolivia and Peru are thought to produce more haemoglobin in their blood, while the Tibetans and Nepalese living at high altitudes in the Himalayas seem to breathe faster. Their accelerated breathing through widened arteries and capillaries enables a higher rate of blood flow. In both cases, the amount of oxygen carried in the blood is increased, with those whose ancestors have lived in these high areas for thousands of years having the best results. There is one particular gene – PDP2 – that assists in the conversion of food into fuel in the body and helps acclimatization to low oxygen pressure. I wonder if we have low levels of this gene, or if, perhaps, we have lived too long away from the rock that brought our family together, the mountain-building 300 million years ago, when rock moved over rock in the Bridford Thrust.

'Trilllalalick wrrrrrrrrrrrrrrrrrrrr rrrrrrrrrrrrrrrrrrrr Trilllillaliiiiirr wrrrrrrrrrrrrr rrrrr rrrrrrrrrrrrrrrrrrrr wurrwurr trickalickalick !' spills the blackbird, in through the open window, into the edge we wait on. Sometimes the edge is made of root, sometimes thread, sometimes elastic. Today it is rock. Birdsong bounces off the sides of our bodies which are dense with time. I feel my lungs expand. During acclimatization, the lungs grow in order to ease the osmosis of oxygen and carbon dioxide, though the ability of the body to function is rarely the same as it was at a lower altitude.

Whether I am here, in this room, out in the fields, or far off in a distant city, I remain at the uttermost. I acclimatize, but I am not the same as before. I breathe in the song as deeply and as long as it lasts. It is a different kind of air. The blackbird changes the colour of its tone, its timbre, as it lilts along capillaries. The bird brings the fields in from the earth and lays them out in the air; chlorophyll bouncing, licking, trilling, trickling. By breathing the fields, I carry them with me. By carrying the fields, I do not ever really leave.

44

Ȳþ-wōrigende

After a long time adrift, it feels good to take the handle of a bucket, to lift a fork, to have both hands grasped on something solid. Smoothing away the topsoil, I upend a worm: flat and light amid the orange storm of soil. I watch the compartments of its body separate and join again, in a motion I recognize. I have been rootless and rooted, measureless and minuscule, flowerless and fully bloomed. I have known what it is to shoot down, low and far, and yet still to be unsteady. I have felt connected, grafted at the nodes, yet loose as a net; all holes; outstretched. I have felt altogether limbless. The earth crumbles in my fingers, breaking off like chocolate. I draw deep inhales, as gnats circle, dandelion fluff flocks, and finally I reach rock.

Scooping the beans out of their compost without damaging the roots, lifting them briefly in air before placing them gently down below ground is my favourite part. This lifting and lowering, lifting and lowering, though it is in the thick of the earth, reminds me of the sea. It is familiar, this ebb and flow, a 400-million-year echo of a time this earth still carries in its rock. A time when this field was a sea, and we had yet to come. When the field was a desert, and we had yet to come. When the field was the bottom of a lake, and we were no one.

And in the sound of this buried sea is the swish of a forgotten speech. The Old English word for 'tilling', *yrþ*, so close still to our word for 'earth'. Lose a letter, shift the stress, and the word becomes a wave: *ȳþ*. One letter, then, was all that split the elements, as if they knew more keenly the proximity of land and water, sailing and sinking.

We had spoken, the two of us, of these lost words. Those times when we had walked together, passing places my father had wondered about, teasing the past out from their names. As I had studied this older language, I could sometimes help. These were rare moments when one as small and inconspicuous as a grain of earth could help one as wide and knowing as a ranging sea. So that as we had walked the lanes, the names had drawn us together; like a letter falling between sea and soil, the space had collapsed between us; we had joined.

But when you have once been sea, it is difficult to be confined, to no longer roam freely over earth. And when you have once been earth, it is shocking to beat against the waves, to have no place to cast your root, to crave a landing. From the worm's path, I lift the foaming loam asunder and hear the word for wandering on the waves: ȳp-wōrigende. And I light upon a poem I once learned, *The Wanderer*, in Old English verse. Though it has been twenty years since the air brushed along my lungs in the song of this ancient tongue, I feel it now against my teeth, I lift my lips apart, I speak: 'Þeah þe hē mōdcearig': 'Though he, sad at heart'. I upturn another worm, unhappy at being disturbed. '*Geond lagulāde longe sceolde / hrēran mid hondum hrimcaelde sǣ*': 'Has had to stir for a long time the icy water by hand, moving along the waterways.' The worm writhes uncontrollably.

I land upon a strip of wood in various stages of decomposition. Like driftwood it flows through the soil, difficult at first to catch, but coming, after it is pressed, to rest. The ragged edges where the soil has bitten it, the white trail of fungi, the yellow fibre through the tawny dust, seem to speak to me. This wood is coming apart. This wood is on its way to being something else. I pick it up and place it in my pocket.

It takes an hour to plant the beans. All the while I think of what else I have planted with my father. The sycamore that marked an early birthday, when the tree had not been much taller than myself. Now it towers so high, I can barely find the top. The time, when I was even smaller than that, that I had wanted to help dig with the fork and he had said, 'Don't put it through your foot,' and I had laughed at the thought and put it through my foot, which bears the scar today. The time I had made some grave error in the locking of the shed, causing him to rage, 'Just when you seem to have grown up, you do something like this'. Or the more drawn-out times, when I had tinkered in the weeds, read or written, while he dug: deep, dark thuds into another realm.

For as long as I can remember this has been the sound of my days, the uplift and down-sway of fork or spade. The crack and crumble of surface. The word '*yppan*', 'to bring out, open, or display', can also mean 'to utter'. And the soil has always spoken to me. Mostly it has been the sound of rising and breaking, rising and breaking. Some things being dismantled, others forming. I have done my growing here. Out in the open is where I took shape. So it is bewildering, now, to be starting again. I think of the stumble with the lock, all those years ago. Just when I had thought I had grown up, here I was, back again, turning into something else.

'*Wyrd bið ful āræd!*' 'Events always go as they must!' '*Swā cwæð eardstapa*': 'So spoke the Wanderer.' And it is the lift and drop of the fork that I fall back on, though it is my own hand now around the tines. I must bear the beat of the waves. I must hold steady through the change.

45

Zoic

I move among the irises. Yellow against blue, they sing up from the pond. I feel their bothness: their rootedness in water, their flight-lessness in air. I pick one, a pulsing indigo, to take to him. In front, a golden flank bobs and veers to the side, before moving behind unconvincing cover. The deer's fawn. I'm pleased the mother has decided to return to this spot to rear her young and wonder how many more years this will happen, and whether the fawn in turn will rear its young here.

As I follow it up the hill, a butterfly flies onto my heart. We beat together, we still together. As I start to feel anxious at having to move it, it leaves of its own accord. As I start to miss it, it returns. Straight to the heart. And the goldfinch cheeps from the telegraph wire and the long-tailed tit flits from branch to branch and the kes-trels wheel over, flashing fleshy white, mercurial in the melting sun. I add some lavender to the iris, and as I pause, the butterfly returns, landing on my heart. I move and it goes; I pause and it returns. All the way back to the house with this flying heart.

'Oh, so you're going for a swim?' he asks, as I settle the flowers into water. 'Where your ancestor lived.'

'Which one?' I am careful to catch the conversation, to hold it still against my chest.

'Grandfather Frank's brother, Ben, he worked at the dockyard.' So many places we had visited during my childhood were, I now realize, the homes of my family. As my father had followed the tracks of their dispersal, so had I, long before I had known I was doing so. Appledore's name is thought to be of Celtic derivation, from the words 'Aber' (estuary) and 'dour' (water). It lies across the water from Instow, where I had learned to swim.

Midsummer's Day is one of the hottest of the year, and of any of the country's summers. I come to the dour. Water sways gold as wheat and I swoon in the heat. Even with such dense sunlight, the water still bites. But I am soon in. As I leave the shore, the person I was decades ago seems to swim towards me. And further back, the person my father was. The space between us all seems at once near and far, like a telescope pulling in and out of focus. With each stroke, self slips. I have become used to feeling different – more expanded – made up of parts that I may not at first have recognized as my own. I have had things settle in me from different places and people. Or perhaps they have always been there; I just hadn't seen or heard from them before.

I have expanded. I am more of my fathers now. My father, his father, his father, his. I have grown towards them and our roots have touched; we are part of the same system. Now, when I breathe, so does he, and so does he, and so does he. And so does the lavender and so does the iris and so does the bluebell, the lamb's-ear, the euonymus, the eleagnus, the oleaster, the barberry, the mountain ash, the Wild Rover rose, the Michaelmas daisy, the sweet pea, the lupin, the forget-me-not, the euphorbia, the daffodil, the dogwood, the Martin's spurge.

The willow, the beech, the birch, the conifer, the eucalyptus, the oak, the ash, the elder, the hawthorn, the apple tree, the plum tree, the wood: they breathe. The blackbird and the chaffinch and the bullfinch and the hawk and the thrush and the long-tailed tit and the robin and the sparrow and the wood pigeon and the goldfinch and the greenfinch and the swallow and the swift and the skylark and the house martin and the goldcrest: they breathe.

And the stars and the planets and the constellations and the meteors breathe. And their names breathe. And the deer and the rabbit and the badger and the weasel and the stoat and the fox and the mole and the vole breathe. And the leaf and the grass and the root breathe. And the field breathes. And the worm and the protozoa and the bacteria breathe. And the earth breathes. And the topsoil and the humus and the clay and the chemicals and the bedrock breathe. And the air and the soil and the water touch and spin and touch and spin so that we breathe. All of them touching and spinning and speaking and singing and soaring and flinging their breathing.

With each stroke, the part that I know as my own evaporates. Possession sinks. But there is still a body and things outside of the body. There is still an out and an in. To strike out and out and out. Arms pull wider orbits, body flattens, lets go of strain. Always the body is calculating: how far it can go, and can let go; how far is too far, and means it won't be able to come back. But I am only vaguely aware of this. I am still lodged in the feeling that I could go anywhere, that I don't have to end. I don't fight the sea but go with it, rising on each high wave, settling into each aftermath. I am an older version of myself. Before I came to land.

The midsummer sun is at its peak. I am a cell being charged: trillions. My trillions of cells syphon the light and pump it around the body. I try to keep as much of me moving as I can. I use my veins. I am aware of time only slightly, in the sense that I know I can no longer judge it. I am as far as I can go now. I can't put a foot down. I can't save myself if attacked. But nothing wants to attack. I am just lifted and put down again, lifted and put down again, all the way, as far as I can go.

I am laughing. The sea gets in my throat, my nostrils, my vocal chords; swims along my windpipe and giggles in my belly. What I thought was water is laughter and I gurgle the moving joy of lifting and dropping, dunking and rising, shining and wetting – sounding. I reverberate.

But I nudge a plastic bottle, and I stop. I end. How do I go on, when there is nowhere to come back to? No harbour, no shore, as 'all the pores of the rock are filled with water, a dark, sub-surface sea, rising under hills, sinking beneath valleys.' I hear the words of Rachel Carson pass through me as fluidly as my own. 'This groundwater is always on the move,' I say. And I am Rachel Carson. 'It travels by unseen waterways until here and there it comes to the surface . . . all the running water of the earth's surface was at one time groundwater.' And I am that water.

I hold not only my own fluid but all of the rocks' of all of the earth; I float on and in myself. I am zoic: containing fossils, with traces of animal or plant life. 'And so, in a very real and frightening sense, pollution of the groundwater is pollution of water everywhere.' Plastic fossils line my bones. The bottle, adrift in the dour, is the seen pollutant, plastic spectre made manifest, but how many unseen haunt the water; how many chemicals through my pores and in my soil and in my rock and in my leaves and in my sea and will I ever, ever be clean?

I flip. I face the sun. I drift. I am damaged, but it is not quite over. Whatever part of me is here is not over. Whatever part of me is not here is not over. Here is a space for salvaging. I am speaking in a thickened voice now. All the voices of the advocates. All the voices of my family. All the voices of the sea, rising. There is still time. I am still. Here. All of me gathers light.

SOIL MEMOIR FOR ST MARY'S CHURCHYARD

When one voice falls away, they all do. The place without words is a dangerous place to linger. Where there are no words there is only rock to knock against. Where there are no words there is no join. Where there are no words there is nothing to bring it back. If it stays here too long, it will not return.

Horizons
ins.
0–9
A   A tiny handful, for the mourners.

9–14
(B)   *As for man, his days are as grass: as a flower of the field, so he flourisheth.*

(B) /C He is rooted Martin's spurge is dogwood is daffodil is euphorbia is forget-me-not is lupin is sweet pea is copper beech is Michaelmas daisy is rose is mountain ash is barberry is oleaster is eleagnus is euonymus is lamb's-ear is bluebell is iris is lavender. As a rainbow, so he flowers.

24+
C   For the first time, no strain. Only the wish to hold, to keep safe; to plant in soft ground and press into him.

    For the wind passeth over it, and it is gone; and the place thereof shall know it no more.

But this place knows him, and the grass takes him to it like a part of itself returning. The Grassling bends into its end. It has listened to its fathers and its mothers. It has listened to the grasses and the flowers. It knows how to hear worms pulse and bark sound and how to be cut and how to be rooted. It knows all this as it lies. And as the rain splashes over its face, as it is carried down, into the falling ground, it knows what it is to reach the bottom. What it does not know is how to get back up.

46

Zygote

It had begun in a tight, light body. Midwinter ice stiffening muscle, bone, nail. When the moonlight had gathered in my crevices, the soil had swallowed all sound. Insects stilled; birds held their breath; the whole earth sighing, *Not Yet*. If there was to be an end, it was not to be then. I had grown through the months, turning, at first, so slowly that I hadn't realized; later, so quickly that I couldn't keep up – into my new form.

Part of me had been dying. I had known that all along; but to live with a dying thing takes an awful lot of life. A whole solar system plugged into the part that is slipping into darkness. And for a while it can work. You can keep the dead part with you. You can carry a strip of wood bitten by fungi, powdered in tawny dust, in your pocket for weeks, saying: *It is with me, the dead thing is with me, and we are both fine.*

At first, the body is only a longing. A yearning for its feet to be roots, for its roots to reach the part that is dying, for its culm to channel light, for its nodes to be the words that join them. For its stolons to reach the part that is dying, for its leaves to channel light, for its flowers to be the light that joins them. Then, the longing fills and hollows, fills and hollows, as the words come, and the flowers fling, and the light. And if they don't come, you can find a way to coax them out. The soil, with its hoard of hidden language, had opened up the ground beneath me, once I had learned to read it.

My father had always read the soil, with his maps and worded tracks. Now I, too, was closer to the shape of it, how it has been mapped and understood. Closer to the breadth of it, to the people who have worked and lived on it. Closer to the depth of it, the lives inside, the other-than-human beings who have relied on it as closely as I have. And as I have processed these multiple convergences, my shape, and the language of my shape, has changed. Now I am a wider thing, with strange beatings. I have swallowed the light of flowers and breathed it out. I have listened to the light of grass and typed it out. My blood has changed. As my DNA carries along stem, along stolon, along leaf, along rhizome, I am zygote, a cell formed by fertilization.

But I have always known that to continue, part of me must break. I have felt the cracks form along my spikelets and moved with the strain, though only part of me has been prepared to let go. For that part, in spite of the sun, each day has been cold and painful to move through. Stiff and fractured, it has begun to feel, without bitterness, that it may have served its purpose. The spikelets edged away from my body.

As I stand now, in Ten Acre field, taking deep gusts from each compass point, each side I face brings a new roll of hill, a new air archive of wood. Here is the open moment I have been searching for, ever since beginning my strange growing. I fix my feet, only turning from the waist. A spiral begins in the body, following the land around. I let the arms follow the waist, as air twists. I remember how, from the fallen beech, I have practised falling. I remember back, past that, to the downcutting of the River Teign; bending from the waist and falling. I remember the cooling of the granite to the West, following the spiral round and falling. I remember the dissolving of the chalk to the East, dropping from the side and falling. Always letting the ground catch me. And always, I remember trying to stay, for as long as possible, in the moment before the end; in the limbo just before contact.

As the end comes, the weight breaks from my head like a bird from its shell, pushing over and out of my body. Feet buckle, legs cave; whole body lowers into grass. The cries from me draw long and coarse, creaking the air like a bow over string. I try to resist, as in the moment of falling I see the hills inverted, trees suspended, fields adrift, like the scene in a snow cone when you turn it over. I see dandelions loom larger than forests, blades of grass bigger than hills. I teeter in the yellow of petals, in the green that offers such soft relief, yet still I resist, until I am in the globes of water that hang from the blades like silver apples. I am in this water, I am in this silver, and I am chiming. No words but chiming. No hope but chiming. No end to the chiming. As, in my last defiance, my eyes flick back up to the dangled hills and the floating fields and the dark trees who seem to catch me just as much as the grass, which, as I come to land, shimmer a loving sea.

AFTER

Where the deep crevice of me leans into land; where valley ends, through rough red and gorse green, all fields meet and give way. In my father's coat I walk uphill, for it will always now be uphill, through worn-down thistle and broken oak, up to Churchills. This, the first field in Ide entered two years ago. The dark hills of Haldon stretched in front, the wide white of sky held above, crows lift off the field and circle: glossy globes of dark in pale light. And I stand, upright like the Belvedere rising before me, now that there is nothing left to fear. It has already happened – the worst – and this is what's left. A skylark's flight, the flooding white, the glistening light: my father.

As the cathedral chimes the morning in, the sound of the bell is timeless, centuryless. Unending, unbeginning, unravelling, unpersoning, ungrassing, unbuttoning: my father's coat stays on. I finger a blade of grass and take his pen from his pocket. I write his name along the leaf. My finger rests beneath the blade. I feel myself through the leaf, the texture of my own body. As I leave, I leave a part of us there.

Back in Drewshill, I think: I have not lost him because I never had him. People are not ours to own. We coexist, if we're lucky. I reach the spot of my summer-rolling and field-swimming. Although there was a joy in it, the sadness was already there, and the fear of this very moment I am in. But still it was a time of becoming, of beginning, of bepersoning, begrassing. Now, it is a letting go. What is it the Grassling leaves here? That awful earthly clinging, that desperate human need to say 'mine' and fence in what was never yours to fence. But I had the joy of coming near – that is what I had – and that is what does not end. Perhaps, if anything, it is even closer, when you realize there is no possession, only ever drawing near.

I lie back in the wet grass and my eyes close into his image. At the sea, where he taught me to swim; in Kenya, in the long savannah; at the races, in the coat I am wearing; young, digging in the garden; old, bedridden, eyes full of questions about what his body could no longer do. I open my eyes to the bright white light: they say that is what you see before death, but here it is only sky. Then, land falls in, big chunks of it, rolling and coming to rest in the valley, tied in a deep knot of itself. And it is no longer about what I know but what I have the capacity to feel. And, oh God, let's all have a capacity to feel. Let our work be towards expanding our capacity of feeling.

I write, slowly, the names of my family on the grass. From my father to the first traced descendant, Mary Burnett, and before her, to Beornhard, the warrior. Sometimes, ink won't settle in the wetness of the grass and I have to wait, then slowly begin again. I continue with the Archers; my grandmother; back to Samuel from Sheldon; back to Edward, first yeoman at Christow. My fingers numb and lock and it is difficult to move. I wait, then slowly begin again. When it is done, I rest on my knees and call out to my father. To my family. To the ground that gives and takes them. The smell of the grass is sweet and full of earth and flower, water seeps in at my knees and I am all dew all field all hope. More than the day is beginning. Morning fire smudged to pastel, dusting over hedges. Sun-gasp. Electric orb fringed by field. That great sun going on. A perfect round, pulsing to skylark's flight, unending light. That great continuing. Glow.

Notes

EPIGRAPHS

[ix] Rachel Carson, *Silent Spring* (New York: First Mariner Books, 2003; first published 1962), p. 53.
Monica Gagliano, 'Plant Communication', *Monica Gagliano Online*, at <https://www.monicagagliano.com>; accessed 19 June 2018.
Enid Blyton, *The Magic Faraway Tree* (London: Egmont, 2014; first published 1943), pp. 9–10.

I ACREAGE

[9] Donald Burnett, *A History of the People and Parish of Ide* (Exeter: Strangaton Books, 1992). Subsequently abbreviated in the text as *History*. Quotations from my father in italics refer either to this book or, as the context should make clear, to Donald Burnett, *The Archers of the Teign Valley* (n.p., n.d.).

[9] William Camden, translated by P. Holland, *Britain, or, a Chorographicall Description of the most flourishing Kingdomes, England, Scotland, and Ireland* (1610).

[11] W. G. Hoskins, *The Making of the English Landscape* (Harmondsworth: Penguin, 1986; first published 1955), p. 95.

4 DAFFODIL

[22] Robert Herrick, 'To the Virgins, to Make Much of Time', *Hesperides: or, the works both humane & divine of Robert Herrick Esq.* (1648). Contains the lines, 'Gather ye rosebuds while ye may / Old time is still a-flying.'

5 EXE

[24]   *Plantlife Online*, at <http://www.plantlife.org.uk/uk>; accessed 18
June 2018. *Plantlife* undertake surveys of wild flowers as part of
their work protecting plants and fungi.

[25]   The description of my first swim was first published in the Outdoor
Swimming Society's blog, at <https://www.outdoorswimmingsociety
.com/long-poem-swims/>; accessed 29 October 2018.

8 HARRIERS

[35]   N. W. Alcock, 'Devon Farm Houses: Part 1', *Transactions of the
Devonshire Association*, vol. 100 (1968), pp. 13–28.

[36]   H. A. Bryden, *Hare-hunting and Harriers* (London: Grant Rich-
ards, 1903), p. 62.

[37]   See the *Encyclopaedia Britannica*, entry on 'lupins' for evidence of
this 'more recent research', at <https://www.britannica.com/plant/
lupine>.

9 INDIGO

[38]   Caspar A. Hallmann, Martin Sorg, Eelke Jongejans, Henk Siepel,
Nick Hofland, Heinz Schwan, Werner Stenmans, Andreas Müller,
Hubert Sumser, Thomas Hörren, Dave Goulson, Hans de Kroon,
'More than 75 percent decline over 27 years in total flying insect
biomass in protected areas', *Plos One*, 18 October 2017; at <http://
journals.plos.org/plosone/article?id=10.1371/journal.pone.
0185809>; accessed 18 June 2018.

[38]   G. Vogel, 'Where have all the insects gone?', *Science*, 10 May
2017; at <http://www.sciencemag.org/news/2017/05/where-have-
all-insects-gone>; accessed 9 July 2018. The article provides the
figures for the Southern Scotland insect catches.

[38]   'Pollination,' *Buglife Online* at <https://www.buglife.org.uk/bugs-
and- habitats/pollination>; accessed 18 June 2018.

11 KULUNGU

[44]   See, for instance, the tree listening project by UK artist Alex Metcalf. *Alex Metcalf Online*, at <http://www.alexmetcalf.co.uk>; accessed 11 July 2018.

SOIL MEMOIR FOR DRUID'S HILL

[51]   The 'Soil Memoir for Druid's Hill' is based on the concept of soil memoirs as described in B. Clayden, *Soils of the Exeter District [Sheets 325 and 339]* (Bungay, Suffolk: Richard Clay (The Chaucer Press) Ltd, 1971). As the front jacket states: '*The Soil Survey of Great Britain* prepares maps showing the distribution of soils, and memoirs, bulletins and records describing the properties of the soils mapped, both from the scientist's and agriculturist's viewpoint.'

16 PROTOZOA

[65]   OuLiPo is the Ouvroir de Littérature Potentielle, or Workshop of Potential Literature, a group of writers and mathematicians known for their use of language constraints. The S+7 method is where each substantive or noun in a given text, such as a poem, is systematically replaced by the noun to be found seven places away in a dictionary; at <http://www.nous.org.uk/oulipo.html>; accessed 18 October 2018.

17 QUARTER

[67]   *World Wildlife Fund Online*, 2018, at <https://www.worldwildlife.org/industries/dairy>; accessed 18 June 2018. This site provides statistics on the numbers of dairy cows worldwide.

[68]   'Sustainable Dairy Farming: Kajsa Petersson', *Arla Online*, 2018, at <https://www.arla.com/company/sustainable-dairy-farming/kajsa-petersson/>; accessed 18 June 2018.

18 RITUAL

[71] Michelle Starr, 'Birds Can See Earth's Magnetic Fields, and Now We Know How That's Possible', *Science Alert*, 1 September 2018, at <https://www.sciencealert.com/birds-see-magnetic-fields-crypto chrome-cry4-photoreceptor>; accessed 29 June 2018.

21 UNDER WOOD

[82] W. G. Hoskins, *English Landscapes* (London: BBC Books, 1973), p. 23.

28 WOODED FORT

[113] A. N. Winckworth, 'Memories of Dunchideock', *Genuki Online* at <https://www.genuki.org.uk/big/eng/DEV/Dunchideock/Memo ries>; accessed 12 October 2016.

34 XYLOTOMY

[144] M. Brayshay (ed.), *Topographical Writers in South-West England* (Exeter: University of Exeter Press, 1996), p. 8.

35 ELK-SEDGE

[146] M. Halsall (ed.), *The Old English Rune Poem: A Critical Edition* (McMaster Old English Studies and Texts 2) (Toronto: University of Toronto Press, 1981).

37 YEOMEN

[154] Donald Burnett, *The Archers of the Teign Valley* (n.p., n.d). The Archers can be found in the records as 'an ancient and honourable race'. 1. This information is drawn from Revd Daniel and

Samuel Lysons, *Magna Britannia: Being a Concise Topographical Account of the Several Counties of Great Britain*, vol. VI: *Devonshire* (London: T. Cadell & W. Davies, 1822).

38 YMBCLYCCAN

[157] The history of Devon hedgerows is mentioned in Rosemary Horsman, *Jottings from Ashton*, a compilation of articles from *Unity Parish Magazine* (n.p., n.d.).

[157] Information on Devon's species-rich hedgerows is provided in *Devon Biodiversity and Geodiversity Action Plan Online* (Devon County Council, 2009), at <http://www.devon.gov.uk/dbap-land-species.pdf>; accessed 11 July 2018.

[158] 'New research exposes secret cocktail of toxic pesticides in hedgerows and wildflowers', *Soil Association Online* at <https://www.soilassociation.org/press-centre/press-releases/new-research-exposes-secret-cocktail-of-toxic-pesticides-in-hedgerows-and-wildflowers/>; accessed 29 June 2018.

39 YMBGEDELF

[160] The 1803 Survey Map of the Manor and *Book of Court Rolls* (D and C Church Commissioners deposit 41/75986C) are located in the Exeter Cathedral Archives.

43 ȲTEMEST

[172] Dennis O'Neil, 'Adapting to High Altitude', *Palomar College Online*, 2012, at <https://www2.palomar.edu/anthro/adapt/adapt_3.htm>; accessed 18 June 2018.

44 ȲÞ-WŌRIGENDE

[174] See Bruce Mitchell and Fred C. Robinson, *A Guide to Old English*, 5th edn (Oxford: Blackwell Publishers Ltd, 1996), p. 271. ll. 2–4

and 5–6 for the Old English text. The translation is the author's own.

45 ZOIC

[180] Rachel Carson, *Silent Spring* (New York: First Mariner Books, 2003; first published 1962), p. 42.

ACKNOWLEDGEMENTS

My deep thanks go to my editor, Josephine Greywoode. Thanks also to my agent, Cathryn Summerhayes, and to others who have offered expert advice: the geologist Peter Grainger; the artist Lucy Rock and the ornithologist Nigel Hewitt. Thanks for the work of Organic Arts at West Town Farm in Ide, the Soil Association, Writing West Midlands, and Penguin Random House's WriteNow.

Thanks to Clive Adams, at the Centre for Contemporary Art and the Natural World (CCANW), whose Soil Cultures project first encouraged my experiments with soil. I am also grateful to the community at Sheldon who welcomed me during my private writing retreats, particularly Sarah Horsman, and to Newman University, Birmingham, for a research sabbatical. Thanks to Helen Davies and Colin Burges, to artist Rebecca Thomas for our day in the field and to the Archivist at Exeter Cathedral for assistance with the Survey Map.

Thanks for encouragement to David Launchbury, Doug Young, Jessica Woollard, Samantha Walton and Karen Butler; for advice, Bernadine Evaristo, Siena Parker and Charlene Allcott; and for encounters: the deer, birds, worms and grass at Strangaton.

Special thanks go to my family, particularly my mother, Polly Burnett; the farmer John Reddaway and family; and my uncle, Harold Burnett. Thanks also to my brother Nick and sister Sarah. My heartfelt thanks go to my father, without whom this book would not exist and who did not live to see its publication. He is ever-present.